THE GLORIOUS ASSUMPTION
OF
THE MOTHER OF GOD

THE GLORIOUS ASSUMPTION OF THE MOTHER OF GOD

❖ ❖ ❖

JOSEPH DUHR, S.J.

Translated by JOHN MANNING FRAUNCES, S.J.

New York

P. J. KENEDY & SONS

This work is a translation of
La Glorieuse Assomption de la Mère de Dieu
published by La Maison de la Bonne Presse, Paris

Imprimi potest:

DAVID NUGENT, S.J.

Provincial, Maryland Province

June 1, 1950

Nihil obstat:

JOHN M. A. FEARNS, S.T.D.

Censor librorum

Imprimatur:

FRANCIS CARDINAL SPELLMAN

Archbishop of New York

September 18, 1950

Contents

Translator's Foreword

❖

On November 1, 1950 Pope Pius XII will define that the Assumption of Mary into heaven in body and soul is a dogma of faith. Such an action is an infallible declaration that this fact has been revealed by God as part of the Christian deposit and must be believed by all. No definition of revealed truth goes beyond this. It does not, above all, create a new belief, a new thing to be believed. It does not add to the deposit which was handed on to the Church by the Apostles and which was complete at the death of the last Apostle. Nor does it alter the deposit, except to make it clear and certain that this detail had already been given to the Church in the Apostolic age. All doubts and objections throughout the ages as to whether the fact of the Assumption has been revealed, are shown by the definition to have been in fact unfounded, however valid they may have appeared to those who made them. The definition grants that doubts and objections have been held in good faith and not through any spirit of rebellion against God's revelation; but it says that now they can be held no longer.

With this relation between the definition and the Assumption in mind, it will be interesting and, I think, inspiring to read Father Duhr's exposition of the theological reasons for saying that the Assumption is revealed. Writing in confident anticipation of the definition, he shows how Christians have become more and more clear in mind about a fact which was always at least implicit in what they believed. Thus we see the faithful pass from thoughtful preoccupation with the Assumption to a serene certainty which the Church expresses in the definition of November 1st.

We are confident that all who love and honor Mary will find rest and joy in the same certainty.

J.M.F., S.J.

Woodstock College

Introduction

❖

In 1925 Father Bainvel, following Dom Renaudin,[1] Father Mattiussi[2] and Father Godts,[3] declared that the Assumption of Mary had reached a point of "maturity" that would justify a dogmatic definition.[4] Other theologians protested this optimism. Among these opponents Doctor Ernst, by his incisive style and the display of an indisputable historical erudition, holds first rank. His historico-dogmatic study,[5] directed primarily against Father Renaudin, concludes with the considered judgment that neither the liturgical texts nor the alleged agreement of the Fathers and theologians permit the statement that the bodily Assumption of Mary is implicitly revealed. According to the Bamberg historian, the Assumption even today must be counted among those pious beliefs which, while not without some verisimilitude or even a certain probability, yet are no part of the deposit of faith entrusted to the Church by her divine Founder.[6] Till the time of his death Doctor Ernst held tenaciously to this point of view and defended it strenuously, first in the "Linzer theologisch-praktische Quartalschrift" [7] and later in the "Bonner Zeitschrift für Theologie und Seelsorge." [8]

The pamphlet and articles of the learned German undoubtedly aroused a certain uneasiness among theologians on the question of the Assumption. And the studies published successively by Fathers Wiederkehr,[9] Deneffe[10] and Müller[11] did not succeed in dissipating it entirely. "Even though we grant," notes Jean Rivière, "that not all of Doctor Ernst's answers are equally decisive, it nonetheless remains to his credit of having insisted on the necessity of a strictly theological method in a matter wherein the imagination too often tends to run unbridled." [12] And after analysing Father Müller's work, the same critic thus concludes his survey of Marian theology: "Father Müller's thesis seems then to be no more than another plea for the defense, as much open to question as its predecessors; it leaves unsolved a difficult question which may be freely discussed as long as the Church's magisterium does not intervene to settle it." [13]

We should be the last to deny the respect due to Doctor Ernst's erudition, which made possible the correction of certain unfounded and premature assertions. But his great mistake—and this we shall have to prove—was to falsify the perspective which dominates the evolution of all revealed doctrine and in particular of belief in the bodily Assumption of Mary. A sharpening of focus is called for. This is the task we intend to undertake in these pages.

We shall first set forth *the theological principles* which must guide our inquiry; we shall then describe *the evolution of belief* in the Assumption which led to an increasingly firm and widespread affirmation of this truth on the part of the Church. And finally, after examining *the present state of belief* on the point, we shall find it easy, we think, to conclude that a dogmatic definition of the Assumption is not only possible but desirable and opportune.

J.D., S.J.

December 8, 1946

CHAPTER ONE

The Theological Principles

Four questions will allow us to make clear what the fundamental principles are that ought to guide us. What is the rôle of the Church in the matter of faith? Under what conditions is the development of a revealed doctrine possible? What are the normal and habitual stages of this progress? In what way, finally, does the Church manifest to us its adherence and the degree of its adherence to a revealed doctrine?

The Church's Function Regarding Christian Dogma

Concerning truths we are bound to believe, the only authority to be consulted is the holy Church.

The domain of revelation is properly her domain. Christ has bequeathed it to her alone. To her it belongs to measure its extent, to catalogue and itemize its riches, to determine the different degrees of adherence that should characterize our belief. For the theologian there is but one decisive question: what is

1

the attitude of the Church on such and such a point? How does she propose it in her teaching and preaching? Theology, as a science, receives the Church's dogma; it does not establish the dogma.[1] Its function is reducible to explaining, defending and organizing it into a coherent and logical whole. Nor can historical science, any more than theology, ever serve as the basis for belief in revelation. As Pohle rightly remarks, "To attempt to solve a dogmatic problem by purely historical proofs, as has been tried more than once, involves the worst possible methodology." [2] Were a fact established by the most indisputable historical criticism, it could never become a dogma, an object of our faith, if it were not linked in the most intimate way with the divine revelation entrusted to the Church. It can happen, on the other hand, that a fact implied in a dogma be imposed on our belief, even when all historical proof is impossible. This is the case, for example, with the Immaculate Conception and the perpetual virginity of Mary.[3] Thus the magisterium of the Church depends neither on theology nor on historical science.

The task reserved to the Church in the message of our salvation is twofold. She must *guard* it in its integrity and *manifest* it little by little in all its fulness.[4] The Church, first, does not create the sacred deposit of revealed truth. It has been bequeathed, entrusted to her by Christ, her Head and Spouse.[5] We may say that Christian revelation was closed on the day of Pentecost.[6] "The Advocate, the Holy Spirit,

2

whom the Father will send in my name, he will teach you all things, and bring to your mind whatever I have said to you." [7] Even before the teachings of the Holy Spirit the Apostles have in a true sense received all.[8] Everything which comes after is no more than development, explicitation. In every age, by its respect for the received teachings, by its horror of novelties, the Church has affirmed this immutability of the doctrine bequeathed to her. Every curtailment is sacrilege; every addition, apostasy.[9]

Immutability, however, is not rigidity.[10] The development of Christian dogma admits not only a more solemn affirmation of revealed truths and a bringing to light of truths forgotten, but a true development, living and homogeneous, analogous to that of the acorn which develops into the oak. In possessing the acorn I possess already the oak, whole and entire, but I do not yet see the tree in its whole complexity, strength and beauty. Many recent theologians understand development of dogma as a simple extension from the formally implicit to the formally explicit. It seems to us more natural and more conformed to the facts to admit a real progress from the virtually implicit to the formally explicit. This theory supposes in the Church the power to discern and to define as dogma of divine faith truths whose formal existence in the revealed deposit is not obvious. In a word, the Church can proclaim as dogma "a truth which would always remain for us virtually implicit." [11] In other words, we admit that a truth which for us is only a theological conclusion, or which does not enjoy even that certitude, becomes capable of being proposed to our faith as a dogma once it is adopted by the Church.

The Conditions of Dogmatic Progress

In order that a revealed truth can be proposed by the Church to the faith of believers and become the object of a dogmatic definition, *two conditions* must be fulfilled. It is necessary, first, that the Church by a quasi-intuitive process, either dialectic or practical, discover that this truth is really contained in the doctrine or the institutions transmitted by the Apostles. In the careful and balanced judgment of Father de Grandmaison, "there is no need to look for an exact proportion between the dogmatic definitions and the research made, the motives alleged, by those who in the name of God declare them. Sometimes, it is true, the implicit existence of the dogma in the deposit will be made clear by research; at other times it will not be so, and the dogma will appear only as a probable or morally certain interpretation of the explicit data of faith. It is the infallible Church which assures us that this interpretation is the only right one; and then, as regards us, there is truly doctrinal development in the full sense of the word. The Church, which has never claimed the power to add to revelation, has solemnly vindicated her right to define it infallibly. The reasons alleged by the instruments of the magisterium so little measure this infallibility,

4

that theologians admit the possibility of error in the grounds laid down for a definition of faith." [12] This intuition which—we repeat—does not depend on theological or historical science, is the privilege which comes from the Holy Spirit enlightening and guiding the Church always. The Church is a social and supernatural entity, which develops and grows under the very pressure of the divine life her Founder has endowed her with. St. Paul points to the limits of this expansion as Christ Himself.[13] The evolution of doctrine and dogma is only one aspect of this whole growth that continues without ceasing. The Church always keeps living contact with the full message of Christ, of which no inventory has ever itemized the contents, but of which we see at least the major outlines. And with the infallible sureness of a higher instinct, which is not shackled by gaps in the documents, nor the uncertainties of the past, nor the ambiguities of a text, and which is superior to the logic of the theological reasons that prepare for the definitive pronouncements, the Church develops the incomparable richness of the divine legacy she has been charged to guard and manifest. Without increasing in any way the apostolic faith she is content to explicitate what she finds there in germ. If there are afterwards more dogmas to believe, there is not more truth to believe, a phenomenon like that of creation which multiplies beings without increasing in any way being itself. The secret worker who alone explains this clear-sightedness, which for twenty centuries has never been impaired, and this sureness, which has never needed correction, is none other than the divine Spirit. "This power, in those cases where the indications cannot be formed into a systematic exposition, of going beyond the natural import of the historical material and the logic which prepare for the definition; this superior gift of intuition which causes the Church to seize with a clear consciousness truths that no demonstrative argumentation has shown to be evidently contained in the revealed deposit; this kind of divining instinct which turns the ecclesiastical magisterium little by little towards the meaning of an analogy, of a fitness in the faith, of a heartfelt tendency in the Christian people, and makes her consequently find the necessary distinctions and the triumphant answers, is the work of the Holy Spirit in the Church, the fulfillment of the promises of the Master, the author of dogmatic development."[14] A marvelous phenomenon, which surpasses any other similar development, vital or scientific,[15] and which escapes the laws of destruction that weigh upon all human doctrine! Yes; "only Christian dogma renews itself without contradiction, evolves without mutilation, remains itself without becoming outmoded."[16]

In order that a truth can be proposed to our faith by the Church, a *second condition* is required. It is necessary that in the light of the Holy Spirit, who enlightens and guides her, the Church discern the truth not only as revealed but as an integral part of the

6

economy of our salvation, as something revealed for its own sake. Christianity can be defined as the manifestation of the Holy Trinity made to redeemed men by the Son of God made man. "To know (in the full sense of knowledge and love) the one true God and him whom he has sent, Jesus Christ." [17] Christianity is essentially the restoration of the human race led astray by the sin of Adam, a redemption of humanity lost through the fault of its head. It has no purpose but to reconcile man with God in friendship and divine life and to restore in all things the order broken by the original revolt.[18] This admirable design of mercy, power and wisdom belongs uniquely to the initiative of God.[19] The plan is realized by the Son of God made man: Redeemer by the blood of his cross[20] and Head of the Church, his Mystical Body.[21] The Son of God made man, however, wished to accomplish the work of our salvation only with the collaboration of the most holy Virgin, his Mother: the new Eve. "Behold the great mystery (of Christianity)," says St. Augustine: "since death had come to us through a woman, it is also from a woman that Life must be born, so that by both sexes the demon may be completely conquered." [22] Without Mary Christianity would not be what it is.

Here, one may say, are the master outlines of the divine message given by our Lord to his Church. The Church must see every truth to be defined as closely linked to one or the other part of this whole.[23] Thus the corporal Assumption of Mary cannot be proposed to the faith of believers and become the object of a dogmatic definition, unless the Church sees it as an integral part of the essential message of Christ. Were it established besides by the most convincing historical documents; even were it mentioned expressly in Holy Scripture—but simply as a fact without close connection with the essential doctrine of our salvation—it could never become a dogma, or profit by a dogmatic definition. No more than the taking up into heaven of the prophet Elias.[24]

It is precisely the task of theology to find out if this connection has ever been taught by the Church or at least if it is now, and as well as it can to put this fact clearly in the light.

The Stages of Dogmatic Evolution

Every defined dogma, as is brilliantly explained by Father Wiederkehr in his work on the corporal Assumption of Mary,[25] has passed through three successive stages: the practice or the custom of certain churches, the adoption or the annexation of this custom or belief by the Pope and the Roman Church, and finally the solemn definition which declares with sovereign authority what was already the faith of the Church and puts an end to all doubts and debates. As early as the beginning of the Church we note this progressive movement with reference to the dogma of the universality of the Christian message. Announced clearly by Scripture,[26] affirmed in the most distinct manner by the divine Master,[27] this

8

truth was not for all that realized, that is to say, recognized, lived, from the first. Some excessively Judaizing Christians denied the pagans the right of salvation, or at least thought that they ought to accept the practices of Judaism as a preamble. The solution to this problem began through the initiative of certain Christians and especially that of Barnabas,[28] who baptized numerous pagans without imposing on them the ancient yoke. In the face of the criticism which they aroused Peter intervened, and far from condemning them, he acted as they:[29] an official approbation of the Pope who made the practice pass into the faith of the Church. The opposition, however, did not yet yield. To quell it, the Apostolic College met in council with Peter at the head and solemnly defined the pagans' right to salvation without having to pass through Judaism. The practice of some churches, the faith of the Roman Church, a solemn definition: here is marked out once for all the avenue whereby dogma emerges into the light of day.

Under pain of stopping, or at least of seriously hampering the preaching of the Gospel and the growth of the kingdom of Christ, it was important to clear up this point in Christ's teaching without delay. Other definitions, less urgent, followed during the centuries according to the needs of the times. They are perpetual proofs of the powerful vitality of the Church and of its keen sense of what souls need. But they will always pass through the same

9

stages, the same phases. The dogma of the Immaculate Conception, the last in date, is no exception. This belief, implied in the assertion of the Fathers that Mary enjoys a complete purity, is made more precise and is strengthened through a special liturgical feast celebrated in some particular churches. Rome intervenes in her turn; she adopts the feast and extends it to the whole of Christendom. Against certain opponents Alexander VII declares that the object of the feast is the first instant of the conception of Mary, and that it is not the purification of Mary which is praised but her preservation from original sin.[30] From that time, in addition to the practice of certain churches, we are confronted by the faith of the Roman Church. Finally, to put an end to every subterfuge and doubt, Pius IX solemnly proclaimed the Immaculate Conception as a dogma of our faith. Belief in the corporal Assumption of Mary is also following the same road, and is going straight forward little by little to the same definitive term.

The Manifestation of the Faith of the Church

There remains for us to describe briefly the way in which the Church manifests its belief. Theologians draw a distinction between an extraordinary and an ordinary magisterium.[31] The extraordinary is the Pope speaking *ex cathedra*, that is, when making use of his supreme authority as Pastor and Doctor of the Church, he imposes on the faith of believers a revealed truth contained at least virtually in the deposit of faith. The same name, the same authority and the same infallibility in its moral decisions and dogmatic decrees belong to an ecumenical council presided over by the head of the Church.[32]

But besides the extraordinary magisterium the Church uses an ordinary one: the habitual way in which she transmits the received truth,[33] endowed likewise with infallibility.[34] "It is by this magisterium above all," writes Father Bainvel, "that the union of the faithful with the Church is strengthened; doctrine is not only preserved by it and made to live in the minds of the faithful and the consciousness of the Church, but also grows constantly in clarity and richness." [35]

The different instruments by which the Church ordinarily manifests its thought, have been described for us in detail by Pius IX in the Bull *Ineffabilis* with reference to belief in the Immaculate Conception. "The sinlessness of the Virgin," says Pius IX, "joined intimately with her high dignity as Mother of God, the Catholic Church, always inspired by the Holy Spirit, pillar and foundation of truth, has never ceased to teach, to explain and to foster daily more and more, with numberless proofs and significant acts, as a doctrine which she had received from on high and which is contained in the deposit of the heavenly revelation." Note with what care the Pope ties belief in the Immaculate Conception to the divine Motherhood, one of the fundamental points of

11

Christianity. The evolution of the dogma and the principle which governs it, the enlightening and guiding influence of the Holy Spirit, are both placed clearly in relief. There follows the enumeration of all the resources by which the ordinary magisterium is supplied for making her thought known as it develops: *the Roman Church,* Mother and Teacher of all the churches, in her living faith and customs; *the acts and decisions of the Roman Pontiffs; the public cult,* for the Pope declares that the rule which governs our prayer governs also our faith. By fixing the object of worship the Church necessarily proposes this object to the belief of the faithful. *The remarkable unanimity of the bishops and the faithful,*[36] *the Fathers of the Church* in so far as they witness to tradition, and the agreement of *ecclesiastical writers,* that is, the theologians, in affirming a doctrine:[37] these too are authoritative witnesses to the mind of the Church. At the end Pius IX mentions the venerable tradition which merits reverence in proportion as it binds a doctrine more closely to dogma and Holy Scripture, whether Scripture be taken only in its context or as interpreted by the Fathers and the Church herself.

At the same time as Pius IX describes for us the way in which the ordinary magisterium reveals its thought to us, he makes plain the submission and obedience which are due it. A dogmatic matter, that is, one tied in with the deposit of faith and proposed by the ordinary magisterium—and according to

Pius IX such was the case with belief in the Immaculate Conception long before its solemn proclamation —such a matter is not merely an opinion more or less pious or probable which one may licitly adopt or not; on the contrary, it exacts an internal and religious acceptance, an act of faith,[38] that objectively is obligatory to the extent that the Church manifests her belief, and subjectively to the extent that this manifestation is perceived and recognized. "The submission which one must actually give to divine faith," writes Pius IX in his letter *Tuas Libenter* to the bishop of Munich, "cannot be limited only to doctrines defined by ecumenical councils and the Sovereign Pontiffs; it must be extended likewise to those the *ordinary magisterium* teaches as divinely revealed." [39] To refuse this obedience to the ordinary doctrinal magisterium renders one guilty at least of rashness, though not, of course, of heresy.

The ordinary magisterium, different from the solemn and extraordinary, does not of course present the doctrine to be believed in strictly defined terms, but in a form more vague, more flexible, more living, more veiled. Again, it is not of course the anathema that threatens the fractious rebel, but the fact that, if not excluded from the Church, he is nevertheless guilty of grave sin as soon as the thought of the Church appears to him in sufficient clearness.[40] Finally, while the Church does not impose a dogma through her ordinary magisterium, still she proposes her faith, which lacks only the solemn definition *ex cathedra* in order to become dogma.[41] Truths presented in this way through the unanimous agreement of the Church can be termed "capable of definition". This is the property which, it seems to us, must be claimed for the belief in the corporal Assumption of the most holy Virgin.[42]

CHAPTER TWO

Evolution of the Belief; Its Beginnings

The First Indications

J OSEF POHLE, following Scheeben,[1] declares that in the first five centuries there is no indication of belief in the Assumption of Mary, neither in literature nor in Christian monuments. "There is a void that no bridge spans whereby we might reach the observed and witnessed event." [2] The notable attempt, undertaken by Father Jugie, the renowned orientalist, to fill up this regrettable gap,[3] is condemned and rejected by a scientific criticism, severe but just.[4] Thus concludes the survey drawn up by Jean Rivière: "For the good of his thesis the author, who promises a long historical and dogmatic work, where the Assumption will be studied under every aspect, will do well to abandon the testimony of the first five centuries, as did his predecessors, or to establish it on surer foundations." [5]

This darkness, however, is not complete. Two glimmerings in this night give hope for a dawn. One, quite feeble and disputed, emanates from a sarcophagus of the beginning of the fourth century, which is still seen today in the underground church of Santa Engracia at Saragossa.[6] We will speak of this sarcophagus in the appendix where we will give our attention to the evolution of Assumption iconography.

A less wavering one comes to us from St. Epiphanius. The pertinent texts are found in the Panarion, [Chapter 78], a kind of herbarium where all the ancient heresies are found collected and labeled. After reading these passages Cardinal Lambertini, the future Pope Benedict XIV, concluded without hesitation: "St. Epiphanius felt doubtful, not about the Assumption of the Virgin, but about her death."[7] Father Jürgens was of the same opinion;[8] and quite recently Father Wiederkehr[9] sought to sustain the same thesis in opposition to Dr. Ernst.[10] A more exacting criticism, it seems to us, calls for a more balanced view.

St. Epiphanius notes that the Bible gives us no certain information about the end of Mary's life. "Is she dead or not; was she buried or not? We do not know."[11] Such is the cautious remark found in a passage whose main purpose is to defend Mary's perfect virginity against her detractors, and to abolish the questionable and dangerous practise of the *Virgines subintroductae* by destroying the pretext certain ascetics alleged to justify it, namely: the living together of Mary and St. John.[12] The very ignorance in which Scripture leaves us regarding the end of

16

Mary's existence, allows St. Epiphanius to venture three hypotheses, of which at least two, he thinks, can find some recommendation in the inspired text. It is possible first that Mary did not die; for "with God nothing is impossible." [13] and is this not hinted at by the verse in the Apocalypse[14] which depicts the Woman borne aloft by wings, escaping with her Child from the pursuing dragon? [15] But even if one grants this simple transfer from earth to heaven, adds St. Epiphanius, Mary is nonetheless a creature, and one may not adore her or offer her a sacrilegious cult, as the Collyridians do.[16] It is possible, second, that Mary died a martyr, and this opinion can find support in Simeon's prophecy, "a sword will pierce her soul." [17] Finally, it is possible that Mary was taken away by a natural death.[18]

In admitting as possible these three hypotheses regarding the death of the Virgin, how does St. Epiphanius picture to himself the survival of Mary in heaven? This above all is the point that interests us. In the case of a simple transference the glorification of Mary in heaven, in body and soul, is indisputable. St. Epiphanius does not reproach the sect of the Collyridians for this belief, but he denies them the right to infer from it that Mary should have the worship due to God alone.[19] If on the contrary— the second supposition—Mary was put to death by the enemies of Christ "she shines with the splendor and the glory of the martyrs, and the holy body of her through whom the Light rose upon the world is

17

the object of highest praise." Dr. Ernst[20] seems to be right in affirming, in opposition to Father Wiederkehr, that the expressions used by St. Epiphanius—if taken in their strict meaning—do not go further than the veneration given to the *Mother of God* by St. Elizabeth[21] or that which the human race will never cease to direct to her.[22] The eastern Fathers, as we will see shortly, happily extend and complete the thought of St. Epiphanius in proclaiming that by the divine maternity Mary has merited for her body not only the moral glory of praise but the physical glory of resurrection and of the Assumption as well. And finally—the last hypothesis—if Mary died a natural death and was buried "her sleep is in honor, her end in her purity and her crown in her virginity." [23] In this instance also, the exegesis of Father Wiederkehr seems forced, when relying on the Apocryphal texts that refer to the death, burial and disappearance of the virgin Apostle, St. John,[24] he claims that *in the eyes of St. Epiphanius* virginity was the principle of incorruptibility and resurrection for Mary even more than for St. John. Nowhere does the bishop of Salamis say that by virginity St. John merited an exceptional destiny. On the contrary, when he speaks of the "admirable and singular death" of the virgin Apostle, he attributes it to St. John's prayer or to God's kindness.[25] What the Church father is obviously anxious to proclaim in the passage cited is that up to the end, up to the last moment of her life Mary remained pure and virgin.

18

But eventually his thought will be resumed and completed. In order to establish their belief in the resurrection and Assumption of Mary, the Byzantine Fathers will invoke her divine maternity and at the same time her virginity.

To sum up: St. Epiphanius informs us that belief in Mary's immortality and consequently in her corporal glory was wide-spread in certain Christian spheres; and while reproving the idolatrous excesses it had aroused, he regards the belief itself as quite plausible. In addition, by exalting the maternity of Mary[26] and her virginity[27] as the source of her glory, St. Epiphanius opens the way for the Fathers and theologians to come.

The Liturgical Feast; Its Origin

With the liturgical feast of the Falling Asleep of Mary we find ourselves on more firm and solid ground. The origins indeed of the solemnity are far from being fully known. In his panegyric on St. Theodosius, Bishop Theodore of Petra tells us that a liturgical service in honor of Mary takes place every year in the monasteries of Palestine. "Once a year," he says "we celebrate the Commemoration of the Mother of God." [28] Franz Doelger notes that this feast certainly does not appear suddenly about the year 500.[29] Thanks to an Armenian lectionary, compiled in a Palestinian monastery and reflecting the liturgical practice of Jerusalem in the fifth century, we are better acquainted with the Commemoration

19

Bishop Theodore mentions.[30] It says, "August 15 is the day of Mary, the Mother of God." And along with the day it notes the place where the office is celebrated: three miles from Bethlehem. At this distance, exactly mid-way between Bethlehem and Jerusalem, we come across a place called, for various reasons, the Resting-Place.[31] Here a Roman matron, Ikelia, built a church in the fifth century during the patriarchate of Juvenal.[32] It may be that the day of its dedication fixed the date of the feast.

Considering only the name given to the solemnity, the Commemoration, one might think that there is question here of a "birthday," honoring the death of Mary and her entry into heaven, like the feasts of the martyrs. Such was the opinion of Tillemont, S. Baumer, Kellner and H. Usener. Such still is that of Father Roschini.[33] This is surely wrong. The parts used for the liturgy—Psalm 132, 8; Isaias 8, 10-15; Galatians 3, 29-4, 7; the Alleluia; Psalm 110, 1; Luke 2, 1-7—and above all the homily of Chrysippus that comments on them,[34] make the evidence a proof that the solemnity's purpose was to praise the virginal motherhood of Mary. We are, in fact, confronted by the feast of the Virgin Mother which we meet as early as the fifth century, though on different days, at Constantinople and in Asia Minor and at Antioch, where after 512 Severus preached on the occasion to his flock.[35]

In all probability the Feast of Holy Mary, celebrated on the 18th of January, passed over from Syria into Gaul[36] at the time of St. Gregory of Tours.[37] The flowering of Marian liturgy and theology in subsequent ages grew out of the unfathomable mystery of the divine maternity.

Mary's feast of August 15 was not destined to remain attached to the Church of the Resting-Place, too distant as it was from Jerusalem. A later liturgical document of Jerusalem, published in 1912 by K. Kékélidzé, tells us that it was joined to the Church of Gethsemani which was restored by the emperor Maurice.[38] In the Canon itself we find no allusion to the death of Mary. It is likely, however, that the feast of the Motherhood of Mary was changed little by little into that of her Falling Asleep through the influence of the memory of her tomb which was connected with the Basilica of Gethsemani at the beginning of the sixth century.[39] The homily attributed to St. Modestus of Jerusalem gives the best example of this progressive change. Father Jugie regards this brief treatise as the work of someone unknown who lived at the end of the seventh or the beginning of the eighth century.[40] So late a date does not seem probable. Even if one denies that St. Modestus wrote this work, the author's statement that he is venturing into unexplored territory scarcely accords with the distinct assertion of John of Thessalonica that already in his day the feast of the Anapausis *was solemnly celebrated almost universally every year.*[41] Even supposing a bit of rhetorical exaggeration here, it must be admitted that neither the feast nor the subject of the Falling Asleep was any longer a novelty at the end of the seventh century. The whole tenor of the work takes us back to when the feast began to spread. The general theme of the homily is the praise of Mary's virginal Motherhood. Time and again the preacher asserts its truth; he praises its glory at length and enumerates its happy effects. Adopting a rhetorical method that became common after St. Cyril of Alexandria, the pseudo-Modestus likes to attribute to Mary all the benefits of the Redemption. With this theme, extensively developed and perfectly consistent with the feast of the Mother of God, there is awkwardly intermingled that of the Falling Asleep. The preacher was acquainted with the Apocrypha. Though he mistrusts them,[42] he borrows from their reports three characteristic details: the miraculous gathering of the Apostles around the dying Virgin,[43] the angels attending the divine Saviour in order to meet their Queen[44] and the burial at Gethsemani.[45] The short extract which follows serves to show how the preacher unites the two themes of the divine Motherhood and the Falling Asleep, though prominence is given to the first. "O the blessed falling asleep of the all-glorious Mother of God, ever Virgin after her childbirth, whose body suffered no corruption in the grave, thanks to the omnipotence of Christ the Saviour, born of her . . . O the blessed falling asleep of the all-glorious Mother of God, through whom we have received the remission of our sins and have been bought back from the tyranny of Satan . . ." [46] The conclusion of the homily is also quite characteristic. "What understanding will be so vast, what word so potent as to comprehend and express the element of holiness and inscrutability in the deeds and praises through which (the Apostles) have glorified the Virgin, and in the mysteries divinely revealed to them? . . . For as allglorious Mother of Christ, our God and Saviour and the choragus of life and immortality, she is vivified through Him; she is associated (note the word) forever with the incorruptibility of Him who raised her from the sepulchre and has taken her close to Himself in a way He alone knows, to whom with the Father and the Holy Spirit be glory and power . . ." [47]

The Liturgical Feast; Its Meaning

From the moment the people were persuaded that the church built, perhaps, by Theodosius II and restored by Maurice enclosed the very tomb of the Virgin, it was psychologically inevitable that the feast of the Motherhood celebrated there August 15 would be modified in the manner in which the pseudo-Modestus presents it, and would be changed into the "Falling Asleep." The decree of the emperor Maurice[48] thus no longer appears as a spontaneous creation: a slow evolution has prepared it. This change is the less surprising as the memory of the death of Mary was closely tied in with the "Commemoration of the Mother of God" which was connected with Christmas[49] from the fifth or sixth cen-

23

tury in the Aramaean section of the patriarchate of Antioch. The Coptic Marian feast, celebrated in the fifth century on January 16, seems marked with the same character.[50] If afterwards certain variant readings in the Coptic record of the Virgin's end separate her death and resurrection by 206 [51] days, instead of placing her resurrection on the day after death,[52] the reason, we think, is not to introduce the new feast on August 15—which formerly was Dom B. Capelle's[53] opinion—but to justify the feast.

Taking account of these various data, we think one can explain the origin of the feast of the Assumption in the following way. Towards the middle of the fifth century, in both eastern Syria and Egypt, the recollection of Mary's death is found to be intermingled with the feast of her virginal Motherhood. A tradition which the Apocrypha undoubtedly preserve seems to have determined this connection. There is not as yet question of a feast of the Falling Asleep properly speaking, having as its special object the celebration of the death and resurrection of Mary. Some of the apocryphal writings, as that which John of Thessalonica and the pseudo-Melito[54] will use, draw the attention of pilgrims and the clergy of Jerusalem more and more to the alleged tomb of Mary that is built into the Church of Gethsemani, the heir of the basilica of the Resting-Place, where each year is celebrated the Commemoration of the Mother of God on August 15. Probably it is this feast, changed by contact with the recollection evoked by

24

the Virgin's tomb and recalled in a more exact and dramatic way by the records of the Apocrypha, which the emperor Maurice approves in order to impose it on the whole empire as the feast of the Falling Asleep. From Constantinople it will be introduced little by little into all the Churches of the East, at times meeting with resistance. From the time of John of Thessalonica it is celebrated in numerous places, if not everywhere, and perhaps in Jerusalem.[55] He himself introduces it into his own diocese.[56] It will be adopted progressively throughout the East.[57] The existence of the feast of the Falling Asleep at Jerusalem about the year 630 is all the more plausible in that it was a former member of the Jerusalem clergy, Pope Theodore I, who by all appearances procured it a place in the Roman liturgy.[58]

The celebration of this feast turns us naturally to a question whose answer is of the highest importance. At this early epoch what was the object of the Marian solemnity? Was it understood as praising only the entrance of Mary's soul into glory, as on the "birthday" of other saints, or did it already mean to celebrate at the same time her resurrection and corporal Assumption? The majority of theologians, following Scheeben,[59] do not hesitate to state that the purpose of the feast, whatever it was called, was the "immediate exaltation of Mary's person in both soul and body." [60] In opposition, Dr. Ernst energetically has resisted this way of viewing it. "The Assumption," he states, "must not be understood necessarily in the sense of 'corporal' assumption." In his opinion the primary and essential object is nothing more than the entrance into beatitude of the soul of the most holy Virgin, a fact dogmatically unassailable. "That this entrance took place likewise for the body is a detail of but secondary importance." [61] How reconcile these contradictory opinions?

We concede that at first glance Dr. Ernst seems to be right. As Franz Doelger notes, the Commemoration of the Mother of God, which Theodore of Petra mentions, fits quite naturally into the development of feasts of the Martyr-saints which commemorate yearly the day of their entrance into heaven.[62] The very names given to the solemnity seem to strengthen this supposition. Such names as the "Falling Asleep," the "Laying Away," the "Cessation," the "Passing Over," or the "Birthday of Blessed Mary," all seem to have directly in view only the blessed end of the Mother in heaven. Besides, St. Andrew of Crete says so clearly in his second sermon on the Falling Asleep. "The mystery which is the object of this panegyric is the Falling Asleep of Mary." [63] And finally, the last indication that argues in favor of Dr. Ernst's position, certain apocryphal accounts, which reflect current opinion, speak only of the death of Mary, and are silent on her resurrection and Assumption.[64] John of Thessalonica himself seems to reinforce this caution. "In short," writes Father Jugie, "the discourse of John is somewhat deceptive as regards the doctrine of the Assumption properly so-called. The author really had in view only the Falling Asleep, and it is clear that for him, who was the first to establish the feast in his diocese, its object is to commemorate this falling asleep. What is for us the chief aspect of the mystery, namely, the glorification in body and soul and the entrance of the Mother of God into heaven, is beyond his horizon." [65] Dom B. Capelle insists in his turn, "We do not know what meaning was given to the feast in the imperial city. But the one it received in the neighboring metropolis of Thessalonica sufficiently warns us to be circumspect and moderate in our inferences concerning this matter. The Falling Asleep of Mary is not necessarily her Assumption." [66] One must not let himself be misled by this first impression, which seems to favor the opinion of Dr. Ernst. This would be another way of acting against the rules of historical criticism. An attentive reading of the panegyrics of the Greek Fathers—of St. Modestus of Jerusalem, of St. Germanus of Constantinople and of St. John Damascene—soon convinces one that the "Falling Asleep" of the Virgin is altogether different from the "birthday" of other saints; it is marked by a *unique character*. Certainly its purpose is to praise the glory of Mary's soul, but likewise that of her body preserved from corruption and raised from the dead. Let us hear, for example, St. John Damascene: "O admirable passing, which gives admittance to the presence of God. For though it be granted by God to all the servants filled with God, . . . *there is, however, an infinite difference be-*

27

tween the servants of God and His Mother. How then shall we name the mystery accomplished in thee? Dead, without doubt? Nevertheless, if in the natural course of events her holy and blessed soul is separated from her venerable and spotless body, and if her body has been consigned to the grave, according to the prescriptions, still it will not remain in death and will not be the prey of corruption." [67] This statement shows clearly that if the "Falling Asleep" of Mary is the object of the feast of August 15, it is a falling asleep that implies resurrection as its final crown.

The Teaching of the Byzantine Fathers

This conviction is notably strengthened when one sees the Fathers labor in their homilies to justify the resurrection and corporal Assumption of Mary. The spotless Mother of the divine Saviour, they argue, ought to escape the corruption of the grave; she ought to rise from the dead. We may be allowed to insist on this proof of Mary's bodily glory, a proof which the Fathers and later the theologians make great use of in arguing *at one and the same time from the divine Motherhood of Mary and her spotless Virginity.*[68]

I. THE CORPORAL ASSUMPTION OF MARY
RELATED TO HER DIVINE MOTHERHOOD

The arguments which the Byzantine Fathers draw from Mary's divine Motherhood in favor of her resurrection and Assumption retain all their interest even today. They have not aged in the least. By her divine Motherhood, the Fathers explain, Mary gave birth to Him who is Life in His own person; she contracted relationship with her Son, the most intimate physical and moral union that can be conceived; finally, she acquired for herself the right to a unique love, which we cannot describe or even imagine. All these are reasons, they conclude, which make Mary's resurrection and Assumption not only possible but morally necessary.

The Greek Fathers delight in hailing in Mary the Mother of Life. St. Epiphanius had already said that Mary, in opposition to Eve, has engendered the Living One, thus becoming the mother of the living.[69] Now, if Mary has engendered Life how suppose that death has been able to hold her under its power? "Since He who humbled himself in her," declares St. Germanus of Constantinople, "was God from the beginning and was life before all ages, it was right that the 'Mother of Life' be associated with Life; her death should be only a sleep, and her removal an awakening." [70] No! "death will not boast of you, because you have carried Life in your womb;" and the vessel which held It "will not be broken by death, nor will it be enshrouded by the somber folds of darkness." [71] St. John Damascene shares the same conviction. He asks, "How shall corruption be able to touch her who has given us Life?" [72] And besides, "since she is the Mother of the living God, it is right that living she ascend towards Him." [73] Further, the monk John Maurope, metropolitan of Euchaita, demands, "Will death take possession of the first fruits of life, and the tomb hold her who by her life-giving childbirth ought to empty the tombs? Certainly not!" [74]

Between the mother and her Son there is the closest physical union. The God-Man, more than any other, received the impress of His Mother. So, for Jesus, would there be a complete resurrection, if He did not make her share in His glory from whom He has taken His glorious body? The anonymous writer of the ninth century, who is hidden under the name of St. Augustine, does not think so. "The flesh of Jesus is the flesh of Mary; I mean the flesh which Jesus has glorified in His Resurrection, since that glorious flesh is and remains identically the same as that which He took from His Mother. If then Jesus, as He says Himself, wishes to have with Him in glory those whom he has joined to Himself by grace,[75] where should His Mother be, united to Him as she was not only by the most abundant grace but by the closest bond of nature, if not in the presence of her Son? [76] She will be there, as are the other saints, through the beautifying vision of God, but also in her own flesh . . . And this all the more because from the time of the Ascension of her Son, our Lord, Mary already has her body in heaven in Him; if not her body through which she gave birth, then that to which she gave birth. Was it fitting to separate, as it were, this twofold body of the Virgin: one living in heavenly glory, the other corrupting in the tomb? No! As long as there is no authoritative teacher openly opposed to me, I will believe that they are united." [77]

The moral union—a normal and necessary complement of the physical union—which in some sort made the lives of Jesus and Mary a single life spent in the same joys, the same sufferings, the same aspirations and the same dreams—this also demands the likeness in resurrection that there was in death. "It was necessary," says St. John Damascene in the course of a passage of magnificent heights, "that she, who with eyes fixed on her Son hanging on the cross had her heart transpierced by a sword, gaze upon Him at the right hand of the Father." [78] And we read again in the same homily, "Eve was condemned to sadness, to tears, to the pains of childbirth, to death, for having lent her ear to the evil suggestions of the hostile serpent; and it was just. But how would this blessed Virgin who has shown herself obedient to the word of God, how would this Virgin united in all her being to God become the prey of death and the prisoner of the tomb?" [79] "Let us enter then into this sepulchre in order to adore; let us acknowledge the new mystery. Raised, carried up to heaven above all the choirs of angels, Mary holds her place beside her Son; for between the Son and the Mother there is no distance." [80]

The love of Jesus for His Mother guarantees for us the resurrection and Assumption of Mary, at least by reason of His physical and moral relationship with her. "He Who has commanded men to love and honor their parents certainly does not turn away from this sweet law. Without being bound by the law He Himself established, the Son of God conforms Himself to it freely." [81] St. Germanus of Constantinople concludes from the premises advanced by St. John Damascene, "A loving child desires the presence of his mother, and the mother likewise aspires to live with her child. It is right then that you should ascend to your Son, the Fruit of your womb, you whose heart burns with love for God; right, too, that God in the complete filial affection He bears towards His Mother should call her to Him so that she may live closely with Him. Thus, dead to all passing things, you have journeyed to the eternal tabernacles where God makes His home; and henceforth, O Mother of God, you will no longer quit His most sweet company." [82] "Would He truly love His Mother," thus the abbot of Sprinckirsbach, Absalom, expresses his thought, "if He refused her what He has accorded so magnificently to other saints? Elias ascended into heaven in a chariot of fire, and the Mother of God corrupts in a tomb! If, after the soul alone had departed, the earth has kept her holy body, why would the Son refuse to the relics of His Mother the honor and veneration that He wished to have given to no matter what martyr and confessor?" [83] No! that cannot be, as the pseudo-Augustine had already observed earlier. "The Son of God, after

32

having so marvelously honored His living Mother by becoming flesh through her womb, certainy has not honored her less in death by saving her from all corruption . . . For, indeed, corruption and worms are the burden of the condition of human nature." [84] Inspired by a similar thought Bossuet will say much later that the Assumption of Mary is bound in the most intimate way to the Incarnation of the Word. "For if Mary has received at one time the Saviour Jesus, it is right that the Saviour should receive the blessed Mary in His turn; and not having disdained to descend to her, He ought consequently to raise her to Himself to make her enter His glory. One must not then be astonished if the blessed Mary rises with so much splendor, nor if she triumphs with so much display. Jesus, to Whom this Virgin gave life, has today rendered this to her in gratitude; and as it belongs to God to show Himself the more magnificent, although He has received only a mortal life, so it is worthy of His grandeur to give glorious life to her in exchange." [85]

Any other course of conduct on the part of the Son of God would be all the more inexplicable in as much as He has besides endowed His Mother with the most magnificent, the most glorious and the rarest privileges,[86] and as there is here after all merely the matter of a favor which will be given to all the elect on the day of the resurrection and which already those enjoy whom the risen Christ has wrested from their tombs.[87]

33

All these considerations taken from the divine Motherhood, which according to the Fathers favor the resurrection and Assumption of Mary, are resumed and condensed by Denis the Carthusian in a beautiful passage from his work on the glory and dignity of Mary. "Does it not belong to the goodness of the Lord to safeguard the honor of His Mother, He Who came to fulfil the law and not to destroy it? As during her life He has honored His well-beloved mother and has adorned her with exceptional grace, so in death He has surrounded her with a unique honor . . . Would He Who honors so magnificently the bodies of other saints have left the body of His Mother in dishonor? When He Himself declares, 'I glorify those who glorify Me,' how will He not glorify in the most sublime way her who glorified Him to the utmost from her conception to her death? At least admit that He Who is liberal towards all and full of generosity does not show Himself parsimonious and guarded with His gifts towards His Mother!" [88]

A striking image, suggested by a verse from the Canticle of Canticles, evokes the triumph of the risen Mother of God. "Who is this that cometh up from the desert, flowing with delights, leaning upon her beloved." [89] Fathers, exegetes and preachers,[90] and with them the liturgy in its most expressive language,[91] recognize in this beloved Spouse the Mother of the Son of God mounting to heaven thanks to the omnipotence of her divine Son and Spouse—"She

34

ascends to her Son but only through her Son," says an old writer—shining with glory and completely filled with happiness.[92]

II. THE CORPORAL ASSUMPTION OF MARY
RELATED TO HER SPOTLESS VIRGINITY

In the eyes of the Fathers, Mary's perfect virginity, even more than her Motherhood, ought to have preserved her from the corruption of the tomb. That virginity is the best antidote against the decomposition of death and a leaven of resurrection, is an old idea that we have already met in the "Acts of St. John," an apocryphal work attributed to one Charinos of the middle of the second century.[93] The virgin Apostle, it is thought, ought to have been as privileged in death as in life. The pseudo-Jerome, from the ninth century perhaps, mentions this opinion again.[94] In the Hieronymian martyrology the feast of St. John, different from that of the other saints, bears the name of 'Assumptio.'[95] In the eleventh century Fulbert of Chartres brings Mary and her adopted son together in a similar destiny. "Christian piety believes that Christ, God and Son of God, has raised His Mother gloriously and exalted her above the heavens; and it is satisfied that blessed John, virgin and Evangelist, who served her on earth, merits a share in her glory in heaven."[96]

But the Virgin *par excellence* merits by her purity to have been saved from the corruption of the tomb by rising again, much more than the virgin disciple.

St. Modestus of Jerusalem insists most emphatically on this consideration. "The divine Christ, Who was conceived by this *perpetual Virgin* through the activity of the Holy Spirit, and was clothed by her with flesh animated by a rational soul, has called her to Himself and in His turn has clothed her with an incorruptibility like His own. And in crowning her with an unequalled glory He has made her take part in His inheritance; for she is His most holy Mother." [97] We find the same conviction expressed quite as firmly later on in St. Germanus of Constantinople. "It was impossible that *this virginal body,* the vessel wherein God had confined Himself, the temple vivified by the most holy Divinity of her only Son, should remain shut in the sepulchre of the dead." [98] And from St. John Damascene. "It was necessary that the Son of God, after having preserved His Mother's virginity untouched in His birth, should save her from the decomposition common after death." [99] In the beginning of his homily St. Theodore of Studium depicts Mary as going upwards towards the eternal mansions clothed in a double incorruptibility, of soul and of body.[100] And more forcefully still the pseudo-Augustine expresses a conviction which all Christians today share with him; "Nothing is more just than that my own flesh should become vile food for worms, nothing easier to imagine. But I cannot think that the same fate awaits the most pure flesh of Mary, that flesh whence Christ has taken His body to make it the body of God; and I should shudder to say so, so strongly does the incomparable grace of her divine Motherhood repel such an idea." [101] One day Bossuet will take up this traditional thought that virginity is a principle of incorruption for Mary's body and of resurrection and glory and will set it boldly in relief. "I say then, first, that holy virginity is like a divine balm which preserves the body of Mary from corruption, and you will be convinced of it if you meditate attentively on what was the perfection of her virginal purity . . . Why, you will never form a just idea of it, you will never comprehend its perfection until you have understood that it wrought in the Virgin Mother a perfect integrity of soul and of body . . . An extraordinary grace has diffused over her an abundant heavenly dew which has not only tempered, as in the other elect, but quenched the fire of concupiscence, that is, not only evil works, which are as it were the conflagration that concupiscence excites; not only evil desires, which are as it were the flame it thrusts forward, and evil inclinations, which are the intense heat it produces, but even the furnace and the hearth itself. In the words of theology the 'kindling of sin,' that is, the deepest root and the most intimate cause of sin. After this, how could the flesh of the holy Virgin have decomposed, that flesh from which virginity of soul and body, and perfect conformity with Jesus Christ has taken away every principle of corruption together with the fire of concupiscence?" Bossuet continues that without doubt our flesh ought to be dissolved and remade "according to the first plan of creation," because it is the "flesh of sin," [102] but "Mary was all pure and she ought consequently to be incorruptible.

"And for the same reason also she ought to have received immortality by an anticipated resurrection. For even though God has set a common limit for the resurrection of the dead, there are particular reasons which can lead Him to advance the time in favor of the holy Virgin. The sun brings forth fruits only in their season; but there are some lands so well cultivated that they attract a more efficacious and prompt action. There are also early trees in the garden of your Spouse; and the holy flesh of Mary is a subject too well prepared to wait for the ordinary term to produce the fruits of immortality. Her virginal purity draws a special influence to her; her conformity with Jesus Christ disposes her to receive a more prompt effect from His power in that she draws it to herself. He has come in this flesh, delighted by its purity; He has loved this flesh even to enclosing Himself there for nine months, even to incorporating Himself with it, even to 'taking root in it,' as Tertullian says.[103] He will not now leave in the tomb this flesh He has loved so much, but He will carry it to heaven, adorned with an everlasting glory.

"Further, Mary's holy virginity will supply her with the disposition for His giving her this vesture of glory. In speaking of risen bodies Christ tells us

38

that 'they will be as the angels of God.' [104] And for this reason also Tertullian calls the risen flesh an angelicized flesh.[105] Now, of all the Christian virtues the one that can produce so beautiful an effect is holy virginity; this it is which makes angels on earth; this it is of which St. Augustine spoke such beautiful words: It has already something that is non-flesh in the flesh;[106] and it holds with angels rather than with men. That which makes angels in this life can well do the same in the life to come; and so I have reason to assure you that virginity has special power to contribute to the glory of the risen bodies in the last days. Judge from this what splendor and light will encompass the body of Mary who surpasses in purity the very Seraphim! So Holy Scripture looks about for unusual words to represent to us so great a brilliance. It scarcely finds in the world enough light for us to trace therein some image; it must gather up together all shining things in nature. It has put the moon at her feet and the stars around her head; and besides the sun penetrates her completely and surrounds her with its rays: the Woman clothed with the sun.[107] So great must be the glory and splendor to adorn this virginal body." [108]

Let us conclude. This comes out clearly from what we have just said: Despite appearances to the contrary, which we have noted, the Byzantine Fathers and their Western disciples intended, on the occasion of the solemnity of her "Falling Asleep," to direct their homage to Mary who is not only enjoying the vision of the blessed in her soul, but who is also reigning in heaven in her risen body at the side of her divine Son.

CHAPTER THREE

Evolution of the Belief; the Apocrypha

IN RETRACING the first development of belief in the Assumption we have scarcely met the apocryphal literature along the way. In the thought of the Fathers who exalt Mary, raised up and taken into heaven, these narratives have practically no place. Belief in the bodily Assumption of Mary appears to them above all as a consequence of the divine Motherhood and of the virginity of Mary, foreseen and decreed by God.

The apocryphal narratives have in no wise created this conviction, though some have claimed that they did.[1] Rather, they presuppose it. And far from helping this belief, they have hampered its growth and called up mistrust and doubt in the mind through substituting a historical foundation in place of the dogmatic one used by the Fathers.

Evolution and Aim

The genealogy and history of the apocrypha that recount Mary's death and resurrection are not at all fixed with perfect clearness. The best exposition of the matter has been given by Montague Rhodes James, in his work *The Apocryphal New Testament*.[2] One central idea of all these narratives is that virginity is the pledge of immortality and the best preserver against the powers of darkness and evil. This is the theme underlying the narrative of the pseudo-Mileto, which undoubtedly harks back to its predecessors whom it undertakes to correct. "Rise up, my beloved and my most kindred," the Saviour is made to say at the moment of raising Mary. "Since you have avoided the corrupting contact of man your body shall escape the grave's corruption."[3]

The oldest texts that we possess of the famous legend, says James, do not go back farther than the fourth century. But the core of the story must have been formed in the third.[4] What speaks in favor of this supposition is a curious likeness of details between the death of St. John as told by Leucius Charinos before 150 in the Acts of St. John[5] and that of Mary according to a vision attributed to St. Cyril of Jerusalem told in one of the variants of the Coptic group.[6]

The Coptic form, which comes to us in four related texts, represents the first elaboration of the original story, in the opinion of James.[7] According to this recounting, the holy Virgin died at Jerusalem before the dispersion of the Apostles, on January 18, and was raised by our Lord 206 days later, on

August 15. The Coptic narrative is relatively simple and moderate, but the same cannot be said of the Syriac version, judging from the fragments that are left to us. Around the central theme of a plot by the Jews against the dead Virgin are developed the most unlikely discourses and stories.[8] The merchants of Syria did not fail to carry this legend about with them and to spread it in Gaul. St. Gregory of Tours was thus able to collect it and give us a quite exact résumé.[9] Gelasius's decree of reproval is aimed probably at a narrative of this kind.[10]

The pseudo-Melito, of the fourth or fifth century, marks a reaction against these extravagances, "which the Church of God forbids to be read or listened to." It aims at cutting them out, purifying and simplifying them. It does not, however, exclude the marvelous from its story. Even more than the Coptic version,[11] it has the bad taste to insist on the fears that shook Mary in the presence of death and of the evil spirits she had to face.[12] Thanks to a double appearance Jesus presides first at the death and later at the resurrection of the holy Virgin.

But in the mind of John of Thessalonica this recital is not yet sufficiently expurgated. His editing results in an enlarged and much more lively story. Unlike his predecessor he represents Mary as quitting the world in great serenity. Yet, in contrast, the resurrection is scarcely hinted at.[13] Briefly," writes Father Jugie, "while wishing to extract from the Apocrypha on the death of Mary the core of truth he believed he had found there, the Archbishop of Thessalonica has simply given us a new story that is *sui generis,* one to which it is difficult to attribute any historical value.[14] The work of the Archbishop was a great success. In the ninth century a monk by the name of Epiphanius records its popularity while deeply regretting it. He considers it necessary to reconstruct the building on new foundations. He will attempt the task by borrowing his information from Eusebius and even from the Apocrypha that originate with heretics. We have this brief account that ends his life of Mary.[15] 'Because of ascetical penances Mary became weakened. And when her hour had come Christ showed Himself to all; and all fell to the earth, seized with fear, like dead men, because of the dazzling light that flowed from Him. And He said to them: Peace be to you! And all, filled with joy, took courage. The angels began to sing hymns while the men kept silence. Then the Apostles also sang. But Mary, falling asleep sweetly, opened her mouth and gave back her soul to her Son and her God She was 72 years old. The angels, singing anew, went away. But the holy Apostles, according to the testimony of Denis the Areopagite who was present, sang a special hymn, though not all at the same time. When the song was finished the Apostles organized the funeral procession and laid her in the tomb, in Gethsemani. A little while after in the presence of all the body disappeared from their sight. And again chanting hymns they returned home.' " [16]

44

As one can see the resurrection is scarcely insinuated.

About the same time when the monk Epiphanius undertook this recasting, we see the legend of St. Thomas appear, according to which that Apostle arrived after these happenings and had the tomb opened which was then found emptied of its treasure. This is the subject of the "euthymiac history" of the end of the tenth or the beginning of the eleventh century, introduced by an interpolator into the second homily on the Falling Asleep of Mary by St. John Damascene.[17] Later there is joined to this narrative the episode of the cincture given to St. Thomas by the risen Virgin.[18] The apocryphal literature on the Assumption of Mary was closed in the thirteenth century by this final episode.[19]

The Consequences

To what conclusion does this enquiry lead? By considering the totality of the evolution of the legend of Mary's Assumption, as we have just done, one conclusion thrusts itself on us. Belief in Mary's bodily Assumption which these narratives reflect, far from becoming intensified with time, is lessened and enfeebled from century to century. The Coptic form is both the most ancient and the most assured and explicit in its assertion. "In short," writes M. R. James, "all the Coptic narratives, except the discourse of Cyril (of Jerusalem), tell us of a corporal Assumption; and all put it on August 15, except a Sahidic fragment which places it eight days after the death of the Virgin." [20] Already, according to the strange and enigmatic Syrian version, the body of Mary is carried to heaven by Michael, and placed under the tree of life, where the soul, transported by angels, rejoins it.[21] While the pseudo-Melito has the Saviour appear a second time for the raising of His Mother, thus recalling the Coptic narration, John of Thessalonica and later the monk Epiphanius omit this scene of the resurrection. And it is probable that the legend of St. Thomas was invented in order to remedy this gap and to reënforce a proof that had become weak. Thus, *while the dogmatic belief in the Assumption of the Virgin is affirmed more and more and spreads, the historical and legendary belief is progressively discredited and weakened.*

It is necessary to add that the condemnation placed by Pope Gelasius on the extravagant accounts, probably of the Syrian version, ran the risk of striking a blow at the belief itself. The pseudo-Melito takes note of this discrediting of the belief and endeavors to dissipate it by a so-called more objective narrative. His effort achieves only a partial success. For, if certain churches, such as that of Thessalonica, refused to introduce the liturgical feast of the Falling Asleep into their calender even after the decree of the emperor Maurice, it is because of the fantastic accounts of Mary's death put in circulation by the heretics and containing things contrary to Catholic feeling.[22] The Archbishop John thought a more likely account would facilitate the spread of the feast. His attempt was judged unacceptable by those more hard to please, such as the monk Epiphanius. Still, the very confession of John of Thessalonica shows us that the apocrypha, far from facilitating and giving credit to belief in the bodily Assumption of Mary, hampered its spread a great deal.

A still more fatal consequence resulted from this apocryphal work: doubt and scepticism. The pseudo-Melito, as well as John of Thessalonica and the monk Epiphanius, had set themselves to give a historical foundation to a belief that is above all dogmatic. They meant to prove the legitimacy of belief in Mary's resurrection and Assumption through history and not through the magisterium of the Church. The result was inevitable. Certain acute minds adopted their point of view and concluded without delay from the weakness of the foundation to the uncertainty of belief in the corporal Assumption itself, contrary to the expectations of John of Thessalonica and the monk Epiphanius. Doubts were insinuated little by little into the minds of even the most fervent. We meet them in the Benedictine abbot of Ireland, Adamnan,[23] in St. Willibald,[24] the Venerable Bede[25] and the pseudo-Ildefonse of Toledo.[26] The pseudo-Jerome, who is Paschase Radbert, abbot of Corby,[27] tells us of his personal hesitancy. In his letter on the Assumption of the holy Virgin he gives us some beautiful pages on the grandeur of the divine Motherhood, the incomparable holiness of the

47

Virgin and her triumph in heaven, at the same time as he opposes Adoptionism; and he confesses that if piety inclines towards admitting the bodily Assumption it cannot however be asserted with certainty.[28] A pseudo-Augustine, in which one can recognize Ambrose Autpert with some probability, is even more reserved. "We believe," he says, "that Mary has been raised to heaven. But we do not know, using the words of the Apostle, whether it is in the body or out of the body." [29] More radically, Adon declares in his martyrology, "The Church with discreet reserve prefers not to know where this venerable temple of the Holy Spirit has been placed by divine Providence, than to teach its place while trusting in data that is trifling and apocryphal." [30]

In his martyrology Usuard adopts the very expressions of Adon of Vienne[31] and for centuries he will be the mainstay of doubt on the corporal Assumption in the particular Churches and monasteries that used him assiduously.

A contemporary of Usuard, Notger Balbulus,[32] abbot of St. Gall, notes in his martyrology the disagreement that reigns among the most learned. In the twelfth century, Isaac Stella still holds the opinion of Autpert which is expressed in Sermon 208, attributed to St. Augustine.[33] And in the thirteenth, Durand of Mende seems to recall a passage from the *Rationale* of Beleth,[34] when he concludes in his own *Rationale*, "A pious doubt is worth more than a rash assertion; however, it is necessary to believe piously that Mary has been totally raised to heaven (in body and in soul)." [35]

In the East, though more rarely, similar doubt and hesitation force their way to the front.[36]

But always it is the apocrypha that nourish this ever recurring doubt.

In the seventeenth century this doubt found a culture admirably propitious to its development in the rationalist and scientific spirit that is the outcome of Cartesianism. We know that this hypercriticism, anxious to refine the liturgy, piety and devotions, brought all devotion to Mary into danger.[37] Belief in Mary's bodily Assumption could only be marked with suspicion by these geometric and rigid minds which inexorably sought out everything in the cult and doctrine on Mary that was not strictly conformed to the Gospel and verified by the most severe criticism. One incident, negligible in itself, unleashed the attack. Benedict XIV has given us the details in treating of the feast of the Assumption.[38] Towards 1540 the cathedral church of Paris had substituted for the hesitating text of Usuard another much more affirmative. In 1668 the ancient exemplary had to be replaced. And it was asked whether in the new martyrology they ought not return to the old formula. Canon Claude Joly spoke in favor of the return and was heard.[39] Two other canons, also doctors, Jacques Gaudin and Nicolas Billiard, fought vigorously against the position of Claude Joly.[40] Joly replied with his *Traditio antiqua ecclesiarum Franciae de*

49

verbis Usuardi ad festum Assumptionis beatae vindicata. Launoy in his turn supported it with all his learning in *Judicium de controversia super exscribendo parisiensis ecclesiae martyrologio exorta.* Benedict XIV relates the principal arguments of the adversaries of the Assumption: the disquieting silence of the first Fathers of the Church, the testimony of St. Ambrose that only our Lord has been raised, the long-standing use of Usuard's martyrology which was perhaps accepted even by the Roman Church.[41] All this, they say, allows one to conclude with certainty only to the glorification of Mary's soul. Moreover, they add, this opinion is better adapted to the names of the feast, the Falling Asleep, the Cessation. Even the name of the Assumption, they observe finally does not prejudice the question. In the same sense Tillemont says he is forced to confess that "neither the Fathers, nor ecclesiastical tradition, nor the monuments of history are favorable to belief in the resurrection of the holy Virgin." But more moderate than his congeners he concludes: "This is not, however, sufficient reason for assurance that (this belief) is wrong. For what we have said does not give us any certainty that God did not wish to preserve from corruption that holy body from which Jesus Christ has taken His own, as indisputably He could have done." [42] He adds, "We do not at all pretend to make ourselves judges of the opinion that seems to be received by the common feeling of the faithful that God has raised the holy Virgin. But we content ourselves with presenting to capable persons the difficulties that can be brought against it; and we would wish that our present subject excuse us from entering into this discussion." [43]

The argumentation of Joly, of Launoy and of others like them obviously presupposes the principle put forward by the legend-makers of long ago. For them, as for the critics of the seventeenth century, the corporal Assumption is above all a historical question. In the name of history the legend-makers of earlier ages pretended to establish it; it was likewise in the name of history that these more recent critics denied it or at least cast doubt on it.

In allying himself in his thesis with this outlook on the matter Doctor Ernst continues the same attempt and prolongs the same line.

In brief, it is criticism, undertaking to establish the dogma by historical science, which is in the last analysis the most redoubtable and most obstinate adversary that for centuries has not ceased to array itself against belief in Mary's corporal Assumption. But the Roman Church has never allowed itself to be persuaded by this spirit nor stopped by this obstacle. It remains for us to see how her faith, with an irresistible drive, has fortified itself in the course of centuries and spread abroad without check.

CHAPTER FOUR

The Constant and Victorious Growth of the Belief of the Roman Church in the Assumption of Mary

The Spread of the Liturgy

The feast of the Assumption was introduced into the Roman Church—it seems under Byzantine influence—a little before the middle of the seventh century.[1] From this time on we will invariably find it in the Roman documents under the date of August 15. The word adopted is *assumptio* which translates exactly the Greek word *analèpsis* rather than *metastasis*, which is *translatio*. This designation is rare among the East, who prefer the name Falling Asleep. Between the seventh and ninth centuries the feast of the Assumption passes from Rome into the liturgy of Milan and of Spain.[2] From the beginning of the sixth century to the dawn of the seventh, there was celebrated in Gaul a "Feast of the Holy Mary" on January 18. The martyrology of Jerome, in its Auxerre recension which belongs to the end of the sixth century, calls the feast "The Laying Away of the Holy Mary." "It is then the precious death of Mary that this festivity commemorates, and that from far back, since the corresponding Coptic feast has the same object under the even more expressive title of The Bewailing of the Lady Mary." [3] Towards the end of the seventh century this festivity gave place to the Assumption. And at the end of the eighth, with the adoption of the Roman liturgical books, the Assumption passed into the territory of Gaul, not only with its liturgy but also with its date, August 15. The spread of the feast made headway little by little in other countries of Christendom. After a time of hesitation, of which a capitulary of Charlemagne still bears the trace,[4] it was introduced into the Frankish Empire by the Synod of Mayence in 813.[5] In the eighth century the solemnity had already found welcome in England,[6] and in Germany, as the approbation of the Synod of Salzburg attests.[7]

But at the same time as the feast spread abroad everywhere and continued its triumphant progress, its celebration increased in brilliance and splendor. Pope St. Nicolas, in his letter of reply to the Bulgars, informs us that for a long time the feast has been preceded by a vigil together with a fast.[8] Leo IV has it followed by an octave.[9] St. Bernard records the very special importance attached by the Roman Church to the feast of the Assumption. He writes: "It is from the Church indeed that I have learned to celebrate that day with the greatest veneration on which the Virgin, withdrawn from this evil world, has carried into heaven the festivity of her most renowned joys." [10] In the thirteenth century Durand of Mende echoes St. Bernard. "This feast with its fast, attended with an octave, is the most solemn of all those that are celebrated (in honor of the Virgin)." [11] In the sixteenth century Suarez notes the primordial importance always attached to this feast of Mary. "It is in some sort the feast that is proper to the holy Virgin. Among all her feasts it has a quite special excellence, because it presents to us the glory, the reward and the triumph of the all holy Virgin." [12]

What meaning does the Roman Church give to this feast that is evidently so privileged? There is no doubt that its homage is directed to the Virgin glorified in body as well as soul. This intention is shown first by the name which, it seems, was suggested by the expressions Holy Scripture chose for telling us of the Ascension of the Lord,[13] and which the Roman liturgy has set aside for this feast. In its official language the Church deliberately abandoned the ancient words Falling Asleep, Laying Away, Passing Over or Birthday of the Blessed Mary, and adopted Assumption. It is true that in ancient Christian literature the expression "he was taken up" is used sometimes to designate the death of the saints;[14] it is true also that the Calender of Jerome designates the feast of St. John as the "assumption," [15] but from the moment that the Church takes in hand the celebration

54

of Mary's glory in and after her death, she no longer uses the word for any other saint. It is the best proof that she intends to honor not only Mary's glorified soul, as is done for other saints, but also her risen body. Nicholas of Clairvaux, the secretary of St. Bernard, declares that by the word Assumption the Church brings together and contrasts the Ascension of Christ Himself and the rising of His Mother into heaven. "The Saviour arose into heaven through His own power as Lord and Creator . . . Mary arose into heaven lifted up by grace, not through her own power. This is why one is called Ascension and the other Assumption. For power is one thing and mercy another. The Creator alone is able to impose His power on nature." [16] The designation Assumption is so significant that the Commission set up by Benedict XIV in 1741 for the reform of the Breviary wondered if they ought not substitute for Assumption some other name such as Falling Asleep, Cessation or Passing Over, for fear—such is the reason alleged to justify this mitigation—lest in keeping Assumption in the liturgy one might be allowed to think that the corporal entry of Mary into heaven must be believed as an object of faith.[17] In the eyes of the members of this Commission, then, the word Assumption appears to be equivalent to corporal Assumption. It is known that they decided unanimously to change nothing.[18] Thus it does not seem exaggerated to say that in adopting the word Assumption, in applying it to the arising into heaven of Mary alone, and in holding tenaciously to this exclusive usage, the Church shows that her purpose in celebrating the feast of August 15 is to glorify not only the blessed soul of the Virgin Mary, but at the same time her risen body.

The liturgical texts reveal, perhaps even more clearly, that the object of the feast is Mary's corporal Assumption. In the Mass of the Assumption, introduced into the Gregorian Sacramentary after St. Gregory the Great but still in the course of the seventh century, the Collect runs as follows: "Venerable festivity, in which the holy Mother of God underwent temporal death without being able to be tied by the bonds of death." [19] Abelard,[20] Hildebert of Mans,[21] Salomon of Sprinckirsbach[22] and St. Albert the Great[23] clearly see Mary's resurrection and bodily triumph in the liberation that is asserted of her in the liturgical passage. Benedict XIV will comment on the text in the same way: "To the words 'bonds of death' one can give no other meaning than the corruption of the body, from which Mary was freed by her victorious Assumption into heaven." [24] The Gothic Missal—from the end of the seventh century—unites with the Roman Mass by its own affirmations. In celebrating the "ineffable mystery" of the Assumption, the Collect Following the Names recalls that Mary "thanks to the Assumption has not undergone the corruption of death" and that her "body had been snatched from the sepulchre." And the Preface: "It is right that you have been received in your Assumption by Him Whom you holily received to be conceived through faith; so that not being of the earth you could not be held within the rocks (of the tomb)." [25]

The liturgical texts that we have just referred to, take care to link the mystery of the Assumption to the essential dogmas of the divine Motherhood and the Virginity of Mary, as we have seen the Greek Fathers do. Thus in the Gregorian Sacramentary: "The Mother of God underwent the death of the body without being able to be held by the bonds of death: She, O God, who gave birth to Thy Son incarnate, our Lord." [26] The Gothic Missal also expresses the same intimate connection. "It is right that you have been received in your Assumption by Him Whom you holily received to be conceived through faith; *so that* not being of the earth you could not be held within the rocks (of the tomb)." [27] The second cause of the Assumption, the virginity of Mary—already set down by the Greek Fathers—is apparent also in the liturgy of the feast. Dom Capelle remarks that the Gospel and Epistle of the actual Mass have already been used in the Mass for virgins or for women especially consecrated to God. Like the sister of Martha, every virgin who vows her life to God chooses the better part, and the Epistle explains that in belonging to God "she finds her true rest." As Father Capelle says, "Everything in the primitive Roman liturgy—even the parts for chant, the Introit *Vultum tuum,* the Gradual and Alleluia *Propter veritatem*

57

and *Specie tua,* the Offertory *Afferentur tibi virgines,* the Communion *Dilexisti*—is taken over from the liturgy of the virgins. And one observes that for these parts, as for the Epistle, there is no borrowing from the Greeks; the selection was made at Rome independently and deliberately." [28] This choice seems to offer us the best proof that the Holy Church has made her own the ancient tradition which saw in Mary's virginity one of the most solid bases of her resurrection and triumph.

Let us conclude. After what we have said about the name of the feast, the liturgical expressions used, and the justification of Mary's privilege that comes out of the expressions themselves, how can one be astonished to see Benedict XIV, while yet a cardinal, assert that it is indeed the bodily Assumption, the glorification of the body as well as the soul of Mary, that is the object of the annual solemnity of August 15? [29] Bossuet determines the object more clearly still in the beginning of his sermon for the vigil of the Assumption. "The holy solemnity in which the Church will rejoice tomorrow throughout the whole world, seems to me to embrace three very important things which, according to the plan of divine Providence, are happily fulfilled in the holy Virgin, Mother of our Lord and our Mother. The first is her death, the second is her glorious resurrection, and the third is the magnificence of her victory." [30] And when today, with the Invitatory of Matins for the feast of the Assumption, the Church addresses this appeal to her priests and faithful, "Come, let us adore the King of kings; the Virgin Mary has today been raised up to His heaven on high;" and when she proclaims, "Today the Virgin Mary has gone up to heaven. Rejoice because she reigns with Christ forever;" the whole Christian people understand that they are invited to honor the triumph of Mary's whole person and not only of her soul.

The Increasingly Clear Declarations of the Popes

To the testimony of the liturgy there is added the declarations of the Popes. The Popes Hadrian I [31] and Pascal I [32] had precious ornaments executed representing the Assumption of the Mother of God. In his exposition of the principal Catholic dogmas addressed to the Sultan of Iconium Alexander III also manifests his thought on the Assumption. "Mary conceived without shame, gave birth without pain, and has departed from earth without undergoing the corruption of the tomb, thus proving—according to the word of the angel—that she was full of grace, and nothing less." [33] Still more significant and decisive is an action of Pope Pius V, done on July 9, at the time he undertook the reform of the Breviary. He eliminated the lesson for the second nocturn of the feast of the Assumption that had been taken from the pseudo-Jerome. This had been read from about the thirteenth century and allowed a doubt to hover constantly over the bodily glorification of Mary.[34]

In its place the Pope put an extract from the Second Homily on the Falling Asleep by St. John Damascene,[35] where according to the current interpretation the Assumption is clearly affirmed.[36] And for the second nocturn of the fourth day of the octave he inserted the legendary account later attached to the conclusion of the same homily. But in omitting here the words "according to the truest tradition," the Pope made it clearly understood that his purpose was not at all to give credit to a legend, but to show by a sort of symbol the faith of the Church and his own belief. This is exactly the understanding of Benedict XIV. He writes, "On the feast of the Assumption the Church reads the homilies of St. John Damascene and of St. Bernard, in which it is said in the clearest way that the Blessed Virgin has arisen to heaven in body and soul. This is an index and a proof that the Church professes this belief." [37]

The Firm and Constant Opinion
of the Theologians

In directing their own thought according to the belief the Church has shown, the theologians in their turn become more unanimous and positive from century to century. At the origin of the great theological endeavor of which we are going to speak, there is placed the work of someone unnamed who conceals himself under the name of St. Augustine. It is a genuine treatise on the Assumption, called forth especially by the doubts and hesitations of the pseudo-

Jerome.[38] With a better logic than had been used before him, the defender of the corporal Assumption links this great privilege to the divine Motherhood and the virginity of Mary. He inaugurates that argumentation which later Duns Scotus will take up to vindicate victoriously the privilege of the Immaculate Conception. "Christ was able to preserve Mary from corruption," he reasons. "He wished to do so because it befits His wisdom as well as His love.[39] Even if this privilege does not befit Mary, nevertheless it befits the Son Whom she bore." [40] And the author adds that no one is to bring against this the law of death that weighs on all the children of Adam. Mary does not come under the law because of her unique holiness.[41] Death is not a punishment for Mary; if she undergoes it, it is solely in connection with her divine Son Who Himself could die but not know the corruption of the tomb.[42] He takes up the argumentation thus: "It seems then that Mary rightly enjoys ineffable happiness in both body and soul, in her own Son and with Him and through Him . . . She who was imbued with such great grace ought to be preserved forever from corruption . . . She ought to live in her entirety, who has given birth to the complete and perfect Life of all. She ought to be with Him Whom she carried in her womb, Whom she bore, warmed and nourished: Mary, the Mother of God, the nurse of God, the servant and the follower of God." [43] The influence of the *De Assumptione* was longstanding and considerable. This was due to the passionate logic of its arguments and perhaps still more to the name that recommended it.

It will be useful to retrace the large outlines of the spread of belief in the Assumption.

In the eleventh and twelfth centuries the belief spread despite the pseudo-Jerome which kept hindering it and which some tried to refute.[44] The belief wins over the Christian world little by little. "Christian piety," says Fulbert of Chartres, "believes that Christ has gloriously raised His Mother and lifted her above the heavens." [45] If there are some who still hesitate, doubters who are mentioned by Hildebert of Mans[46] and J. Beleth,[47] by far the greater number believe it piously.[48] "Yes," says Hugh of St. Victor, "she who has conceived without spot and borne without pain, who became mother without loss of virginity, who placed God in the world, who died without suffering, was also preserved from corruption; and we believe she lives in heaven with her body." [49] "It is piously believed." These words seem to sum up the state of the belief at the time when Scholasticism is about to spread abroad.

The masters of theology are favorable, on the whole, to belief in the corporal Assumption. After St. Albert the Great has reviewed the liturgy, Holy Scripture and the Fathers, and expounded the arguments from its fitness, he concludes: "These reasons and this testimony give us certainty that the blessed Mother of God has been raised to heaven in body and soul above the choirs of angels. We are convinced that such is the truth." [50] For St. Thomas it is a truth solidly supported;[51] and it is his own belief.[52] St. Bonaventure is of exactly the same mind. For him there is no doubt about the Assumption; he asserts it and proves it.[53]

This labor of thought, going hand in hand with the spread of the liturgical feast considered by Sicard of Cremona as the greatest of the Virgin's feasts,[54] naturally strengthened souls more and more in their belief in the Assumption. Durand of Mende records this progress at the end of the thirteenth century. He not only notes that Mary's privilege is in fact admitted, but he declares that despite the doubt which persists with some it ought to be piously believed.[55]

In the fifteenth century we again find belief in the Assumption fortified and widespread. In a martyrology transcribed in 1412 at Haguenau in Alsace one reads this note regarding the text of Usuard: "But all the holy doctors say that Mary has gone up into heaven with her body and her soul. Only the (pseudo-) Jerome says nothing with certainty about the Assumption." [56] On his part St. Antoninus of Florence observes that the Assumption has become an object of universal belief. "It is admitted by the faithful and the doctors." [57] An event which upset the whole intellectual and ecclesiastical world of Paris is still more significant than the statement of the Bishop of Florence for ascertaining the state of belief in the Assumption at the end of the fifteenth century.

On August 15, 1497 the Dominican John Morcelle, bachelor in theology, preached a very bold sermon in the course of which he stated, among other errors, that belief in the Assumption could be withheld without committing mortal sin, since it was not an article of faith. Aroused, the University of Paris together with the Bishop imposed an immediate retractation on the too daring preacher. On August 23 John Morcelle submitted, and renounced four condemned propositions. This is what he has to say about the third. "3. We are not held to believe under pain of mortal sin that the Virgin has been assumed into Paradise in body and soul, because this is not an article of faith. This proposition, as it stands, is *temerarious*, scandalous, against the common belief, belittling to the good devotion of the Christian people towards the most excellent and blessed Virgin Mary, false and heretical." [58]

The distance traversed since the ninth century is considerable. The continuity of the belief's progress escapes us, it is true, as does the growth of every living thing; but after intervals of varying lengths the fact of progress makes itself known to any attentive observer. Notger, called the Stammerer, as well as Autpert, the pseudo-Augustine of Sermon 208, testify that the corporal Assumption is still a matter of debate among theologians.[59] At the end of the eleventh century it has become a "pious belief" and such still is the opinion of St. Thomas, St. Bonaventure, Walter of Château-Thierry[60] and the Franciscan

Bartholomew of Bologna.[61] Towards the end of the thirteenth century Durand of Mende ventures that it *"must* be piously believed" and in the fifteenth century the belief is considered obligatory without its being defined. This stage of evolution in the doctrine of the Assumption is admirably reflected at the end of the fifteenth century in the second sermon on the Assumption by Gabriel Biel.[62] It merits a summary. The feast of the Assumption, he observes, is not only the most excellent and radiant among the feasts of the saints but also among the solemnities of Mary.[63] The object of the feast is clearly indicated in the Gregorian Collect *Veneranda.* . . . Mary has been preserved, not indeed from death, but from the triple bond of death: the suffering usually endured by the dying, the attack of evil spirits, and the decomposition of the body.[64] This truth ought to be believed piously.[65] We have besides the most convincing reasons for believing in this preservation and this resurrection, drawn either from the Virgin herself, or from her divine Son, or from our personal advantage.[66]

Her leaving the world ought to answer to her entering the world.[67] Immaculate in her Conception and spotless in her life, it is becoming that the Virgin be preserved, not from death, but from the decomposition of the tomb which is properly the punishment for sin. United as she was during her life to her divine Son by the closest union and associated with all the mysteries of His life, how would she be separated from Him after death? [68] Her virginity, con-

65

firmed by her admirable Motherhood, calls for the same privilege. For this body which has given birth without corruption to the body of Christ cannot become the prey of worms.[69] Lastly on account of her Motherhood the very Resurrection of the Son entails that of the mother. For if it is true that the nature of the mother is that of the son, it follows that the nature of the son is also that of the mother. Not, to be sure, by a personal and substantial union, but by a union of bodily nature. A unity, marvelous in this case, that grace and nature conspired to realize.[70]

From the Son's part the Assumption is equally necessary. It is called for by His justice, wisdom and love.[71] It is certain—and this remark is judicious and profound—that Christ by His death has won a total victory over sin and its consequences. Now if Mary, who above all should benefit by this grace, has not been raised, then Christ has not won in any instance a total triumph over sin and the demon. This would look like defeat.[72] His Wisdom, at the same time sweet and strong, demands the same privilege for Mary. For He who with power has broken the pride of the rebellious angels and has made them undergo a merciless punishment, ought with kindness to raise above the angels in her whole person she who on earth has been more pure than the angels. Besides, a wise architect is not content to adorn only the interior when he builds his home; he cares for the outside as well. Thus the Son ought to glorify both in body and in soul the home His Father has made for Him.

And finally love, the love that He has enjoined on all children towards their mother, the love that He has practised so wonderfully Himself during His life even among the agonies of death, demands that the Son give Mary the glory of resurrection. Yes, "it is pious to believe that He has crowned her in death also with a unique grace." [73]

And finally, the resurrection of Mary is necessary for ourselves. It satisfies our filial piety which could not bear to see other saints honored more magnificently than the Mother of God. It maintains and strengthens our faith in the resurrection, better than the victory of Jesus over death. For Jesus, after all, is God, while Mary is purely human.[74] It favors lastly our confidence in our Mediatrix with God. For even as the Son shows His wounds to the Father of heaven to intercede for us, so Mary shows the Son the breast at which He was carried to intercede for us with Him.[75]

These reflections, which briefly summarize all previous tradition, are found again among the great theologians of the sixteenth century. Carried forward by an agreement that becomes more assured and unanimous from day to day, they add that belief in the bodily Assumption must be admitted under pain of rashness. Let us hear Suarez formulate his thought, which is on the whole the common thought, expressed with his usual clearness.

"Without doubt the doctrine of the Assumption is not a matter of faith, as Catharinus maintained; but against what Tostado thought it is not merely the more probable opinion. For here *we find before us a matter of doctrine admitted by the whole Church.* Thus, no pious Catholic can put it in doubt nor deny it without rashness." Melchior Cano will say: without *brazen* rashness.[76] Besides, he adds elsewhere, it is on a par with the doctrine of the Immaculate Conception and is *almost* a matter of faith.[77] And if under the impulse of the Holy Spirit the universal agreement is still more intensified, this will be enough to make it definable as a dogma of our faith.[78] With the exception of Catharinus,[79] who exaggerates in the matter, and of one or another minimizing theologian who still doubts the Assumption,[80] such is the outlook of all the theologians, of a Soto or a Billuart, or of Benedict XIV.[81] So we ascertain that the belief has become more consistent and universal day by day from the time of the pseudo-Augustine to that of Suarez. St. Peter Canisius records the unceasing progress. "The opinions and hesitations of some," he writes, "do not stop us from now believing in the bodily Assumption of Mary more resolutely, from affirming it more plainly and from professing it more openly—together with the Church—than was done in the first centuries of Christianity. For the Church acquires wisdom through the ages, and she receives and manifests ever increasingly the light of truth, under the guidance of the Holy Spirit Who rules and teaches her." [82]

How explain this assurance which is not met with

in the thirteenth century? There are, in short, no new arguments. Suarez is content to resume what the Fathers, St. John Damascene and the pseudo-Augustine have said on the matter.[83] But what is new is the more clear and universal affirmation of the ordinary magisterium of the Church as expressed by the splendor given to the feast of August 15, by the almost universal agreement among doctors and theologians, by the decision of the University of Paris, which proscribed the contrary proposition in 1497 as rash, scandalous, opposed to common belief and tending to belittle the proper devotion of the Christian people,[84] by preachers of the stature of St. Bernardine of Sienna,[85] by the conviction of the faithful. The action of Pius V—the introduction into the Breviary of clearer declarations and the elimination of a text which favored doubt—is perhaps no stranger to the spread of the belief.

De Bérulle and the whole French school[86] of the seventeenth century bow to this unanimous feeling, together with the learned Cardinal Bellarmine[87] and the careful Théophile Raynaud.[88]

For the eighteenth century let it be enough to point out two lights of this period, Benedict XIV and St. Alphonsus Liguori. Not content merely to recall the language of the Fathers, Cardinal Lambertini thinks it even more important to disclose the true thought of the Church in the liturgy. For him the thought is so clear as to leave no doubt. For if the Church has come to reserve the name of Assumption

69

for the feast of August 15, what she wishes to propose to the faithful is the glorification not only of Mary's soul, but of her body also. Besides, let one read the homilies of the Byzantine Fathers carefully, and one will recognize that in their mouth the term Falling Asleep is equivalent to Assumption.[89] He concludes with Thomassine that this conviction has sent such deep roots into the souls of the faithful "that it would be easier to destroy human society than to abolish this belief." [90] The thought of St. Alphonsus Liguori is equally certain. His argumentation leads one to suppose that in his time belief in the Assumption was more universal than that in the Immaculate Conception. "If the common agreement of the faithful teaches us *with certainty about the sanctification of Mary in the womb of her mother and of her glorious Assumption into heaven in body and soul, why does not this same universal agreement* give us every security regarding the Immaculate Conception?" [91] The contemporaries of St. Alphonsus, Sedlmayr[92] and Trombelli,[93] share this same certainty. These writers, and others, agree in declaring that the corporal Assumption of Mary cannot be denied without rashness, that is, without grave disobedience to the doctrinal authority of the Church.

Progress of the Belief Shown by Christian Art

Christian art, in its own way, manifests the constant progression of belief in the corporal Assumption of Mary. It is sufficient for the moment to note the principal phases in the development of this iconography. The present sketch will be completed in the appendix attached to this study. Very rarely in antiquity, it seems, does the Assumption figure among the religious subjects treated by Byzantine art; we note the sarcophagus of Santa Engracia at Saragossa (?)[94] and an embroidered cloth of the Cathedral of Sens, from the seventh or eighth century.[95] It is only at the beginning of the tenth century that the miniaturists of the Ottonian epoch begin to draw it out from the scene of the Falling Asleep bequeathed to the West by Byzantium. On the great door of Senlis and of Notre Dame of Paris the resurrection of Mary, conceived according to the data of the Apocrypha, attracts attention amid the great monumental art of the Middle Ages. Little by little the risen Virgin vanishes from the sight of the Apostles. And while they look closely into the empty tomb, where they see only the linens and roses and lilies, the Virgin mounts towards heaven, carried by angels—[96] according to Titian and Rubens—or already seated beside her divine Son she is crowned by Him—according to Dürer and Raphael. At last abandoning the inspiration suggested by the Apocrypha, art undertakes to reproduce the vision that shines in the depths of souls. This will be the definitive formula. Titian originated it in his fresco for the Chapel of St. Zeno in the Church of the Crusaders in Venice. Surrounded by a band of little angels Mary rises to-

71

wards God in irresistible flight with her eyes open widely on the Uncreated Glory. At almost the same time as the Immaculate Conception, the Assumption reaches the term of its artistic evolution. Guido Reni, Pacheco or Murillo, Nicolas Poussin or Philippe de Champaigne, and many others after them, will do no more than translate in their own idiom the inspired concept of the painter of Venice. Carried by angels or lifting herself up with spontaneous motion, we always see Mary arising in the serenity of space, freed from every reminder of earth. We note that this art is developed only under the guidance and with the approbation of the Popes and the Bishops. It is unfolded in the Churches before the eyes of the faithful like a support and a stimulant of their piety. This is the proof that the Church here acknowledges the inspiration as her own. She uses this image and encourages it to express and make concrete her own thought.

*　　*　　*

The conclusions of this long enquiry into the evolution through the centuries of belief in the bodily Assumption of Mary come forward spontaneously. Contrary to the statement of certain writers, the apocryphal literature does not play any decisive role in the development of this belief. The Church never uses it as a support or foundation of her thought. And if in art or even in the liturgy she has borrowed from it discreetly, it is solely as a symbol for expressing her

72

own conviction. Far from favoring adherence to Mary's privilege, the Apocrypha have in fact aroused and entertained doubt and scepticism in minds regarding it, by trying to establish Mary's corporal Assumption through history. The pseudo-Augustine as well as Adon of Vienne and Usuard abstain from judging in order not to yield to such frivolous and vain story-tellers.

In the course of our exposition the reader has been able to note that Holy Scripture holds but a secondary place in the argumentation of the Fathers and theologians. In celebrating the glories of the risen Mary the Fathers, however, like to comment on certain texts, such as Psalm 131, 8: "Arise, O Lord, into thy resting place; thou and *the ark,* which thou hast sanctified." and Psalm 44, 10: "The daughters of kings have delighted thee in thy glory. *The queen stood on thy right hand in gilded clothing.*" Or again three texts taken from the Canticle of Canticles: 3, 6: "Who is she that goeth up by the desert, as a pillar of smoke of aromatical spices, of myrrh, and frankincense, and of all the powders of the perfumer?" 6, 9: "Who is she that cometh forth as the morning rising, fair as the moon, bright as the sun, terrible as an army set in array?" 8, 5: "Who is this that cometh up from the desert, flowing with delights, leaning upon her beloved?" Referring to the Assumption, Pope Alexander III recalls, the "Hail, full of grace" of the Annunciation; and certain writers comment on two verses of the Apocalypse, 11, 19: "And the temple of

God was opened in heaven: and *the ark of his testament* was seen in his temple;" and 12, 1: "And a great sign appeared in heaven: a Woman clothed with the sun, and the moon under her feet, and on her head a crown of twelve stars." [97] But from the way in which these texts are used and commented on, it appears that they do not serve to *establish* the Assumption but to *illustrate* the belief. Scripture, even with the comments of the Fathers, does not seem to us to give a true proof of Mary's great privilege. We think there is a *single exception*, the text of Genesis 3, 15, not by itself but as clarified by the ordinary magisterium, which establishes a strict connection between the Redeemer and His Mother. Only this passage, we think, offers a scriptural basis for belief in the Assumption. We will expound this proof in the next chapter.

The principal support of belief in the Assumption is the conviction of the Church, expressed by the liturgy of the feast of August 15, and the increasingly unanimous agreement of the Church teaching and the Church taught. From Abelard to Benedict XIV, passing through Dominic Soto and Suarez, it is always this argument that is put first for accrediting Mary's privilege. And the liturgical texts tell us that if the Church affirms this privilege with ever more firmness, it is because she sees it *virtually included* in Mary's great prerogative: *her virginal Motherhood*. Doubtless this knowledge would remain obscure and confused for a long time, even for centu-

74

ries, but—as we have said in the first part of this exposition—that is enough to permit a true dogmatic development. Guided and enlightened by the divine Spirit, Who never fails to assist her, and growing in age and wisdom as did her Founder, the Church has become ever more clearly conscious of this truth, as of many others. Understand us well. We do not say —and this is of capital importance—that the theologian can conclude to the Assumption of Mary from the *abstract* notion of the divine Motherhood; but we say that the *Church of Christ*, thanks to a light that is hers alone, can discern clearly in the *concrete* notion of Mary's Motherhood—such as Christ conceived it and wished it to be, with its principles and consequences—the privilege of the corporal Assumption. The Church has not only recognized it; she has affirmed it and honors it with a special cult. This affirmation and cult have gone on progressing and expanding without pause since the day when Rome adopted the eastern feast of August 15.

Before we conclude, it remains to be seen what is the state of this belief today.

❖

CHAPTER FIVE

Present State of Belief in the Assumption

FROM THE TIME of St. Alphonsus Liguori the thought of the Church on the corporal Assumption of Mary has been clearly affirmed. Belief in it has been expressed at least as clearly as belief in the Immaculate Conception. Far from weakening or lessening, this belief has only increased up to our day. Today the ordinary magisterium not only enjoins it through all its instruments, but has linked it with the divine Motherhood the source of all of Mary's glories, in still another way than in the past. We shall speak first of the affirmation of the belief, and then of its new justification.

The Affirmation of the Belief

To the testimony of Pascal I, Alexander III, Pius V and Benedict XIV there has just recently been joined that of His Holiness Pius XII at present reigning. The Encyclical on the Mystical Body, June 29, 1943, ends with this invitation, which is addressed to all the faithful: "Let us beseech the most holy Mother of all the members of Christ,[1] to whose heart We have with confidence consecrated all men and *who now in heaven shines in the glory of her body and soul* and reigns with her Son, that she will multiply her entreaties with Him, so that her most efficacious patronage may protect the Church today as formerly."

The bishops and the Christian people are today practically at one in the same belief. Among the manifestations from the episcopate, the "postulatum" of February 23, 1870, signed by 200 Bishops of the Vatican Council and asking for the definition of Mary's bodily Assumption, is one of the most impressive. It reads: "In this postulatum it is asked that the holy Council of the Vatican explain, and expressly and solemnly define that Mary with her spotless soul and virgin body is enthroned in heaven at the right hand of the Son of God, as our most powerful mediatrix, in order to give the greatest honor to the Son of God and the Mother of God, and indescribable joy to all faithful Christians." [2] Since the time of this petition up to 1920, about 260 other Bishops from the most diverse countries have come forward to strengthen this appeal.[3] Italy and France hold the first place in this desire to see Mary's privilege recognized by a definition. Germany, on the contrary, Austria, England and Switzerland still keep a silent reserve.[4] In 1934 after five years of propaganda the *Forze Italiane* have been able to record the names of 600 Archbishops and Bishops approving the world-wide plebiscite that asks for the definition of the Assumption.[5]

The faithful, in their turn, are caught up by the same movement. In his pamphlet J. Ernst attests the fact while deploring it. He writes: "In recent years pious laymen have in large measure taken an interest in the definition of the corporal Assumption . . . For several years there has been founded in France an organization of prayer for obtaining from heaven the favor of a solemn definition." And he adds that "the propaganda means to pass the frontier and extend itself especially into Bavaria. The international congresses held in honor of Mary have expressed the same intention and the same hope."[6] It is certain that no truly faithful believer will ever accept the idea that the Virgin Mary's body, the august tabernacle of the Word made flesh, could become the prey of worms, or that it remains somewhere shrouded in silence and indifference. "This is an undeniable fact," writes Livius, "that the idea of Mary living in heaven in the integrity of her person, with her divine Son, is—if we may so express it—natural to the Catholic heart and mind. And far from presenting any difficulty, it is so obvious that, once given the teachings of the Faith regarding Mary, it is scarcely possible to think otherwise. Further, the idea of the Assumption is so fruitful for piety that it gives believers a sense of confidence and very special joy."[7] And Scheeben: "The very thought of possible corruption of the virginal body of Mary shakes the heart of the faithful with a thrill of horror." [8] This feeling is observed even in well thinking Protestant circles. An interesting testimony to this state of mind is that which Cordula Wohler gives during her correspondence with Alban Stolz. "I think it impossible that the body which carried the Son of God could be dissolved by death. This holy body, this Temple of God could not and ought not be decomposed in the ground. The honor of God demands it. This is why the Mother of God must have been received into heaven in body and soul. This belief is imposed as a certainty on whomsoever realizes the meaning of the terms *heavenly noblesse, Mother of God.*" [9]

J. Ernst is forced to minimize the importance of the postulatum signed by the members of the council.[10] He observes that they represent only a small part of all assembled, and that they have died without finding heirs of their thought. In fact, the moral influence of this petition was and remains considerable. It had contributed in large part to the creation of unanimity among theologians and ecclesiastical writers in affirming the corporal Assumption. In his article on the definability of Mary's Assumption Father Deneffe enumerates at least 18 theologians since Scheeben who have come out plainly in favor of it.[11] To be certain of this unanimity it is enough to run through the theological manuals used in diocesan seminaries and the scholasticates of religious orders with the approval of the Church. Scarcely a dissenting voice, like that of F. X. Kraus or

79

J. Ernst, is still raised to protest, and to interpret the Assumption solely in the sense of the glorification of Mary's soul. In one way or another all theologians today admit with Father Sertillanges, "We believe then that the 'way of all flesh' has come to an end in whatever concerns the Virgin; the epic of the worm has not been chanted. We sing another song; and it is *Magnificat*, not a *De Profundis*, that bursts upon us above this tomb." [12]

Out of this universal accord—of the Pope, of the Bishops and the faithful, of the liturgy and theology, of the Eastern and Western Church,[13] of dogmatic treatises and religious art—it results that we are confronted "by the most firm faith of the Church, expressed in venerable tradition, in the constant feeling of the Church, in the unanimity of the Bishops and the Catholic faithful throughout the world, in important actions and constitutions" of the Popes, as was said by Pius IX in describing the period that preceded his definition of the Immaculate Conception. It must be concluded that the ordinary magisterium proposes the doctrine of the corporal Assumption, not as a probable opinion that may licitly be admitted or rejected, but in an imperative and authoritative way. The corporal Assumption is completely a part of the Church's Faith. It is linked in the most intimate way with the deposit that Christ has confided to His Spouse. It *must* be piously believed,[14] as coming plainly from the ordinary magisterium. If this point be once admitted, the definability of the

Assumption no longer causes difficulty. For the extraordinary magisterium can define whatever the ordinary magisterium proposes to the faithful in a less absolute manner. With Father Bainvel we think that the Assumption is quite ready for a definition.

The Belief Linked to the Idea of the "New Eve"

We have said in explaining the theological principles on which we lean that for a truth or a fact to be definable it must have a close connection with the fundamental truths of our faith. But only the Church, enlightened and guided by the Holy Spirit, is the judge in such a matter.

We have seen how a long tradition, which goes back to the Greek Fathers, and by which the Church has been and still is inspired in the liturgy of the Assumption, links Mary's bodily Assumption to her dignity as Mother of God, which dignity is increased by her virginity; and thus links it to one of the central dogmas of Christianity. Benedict XIV, Suarez and the pseudo-Augustine, who himself merely improves upon his inheritance, unite on this point with the Gregorian Sacramentary and the Gothic Missal.

But the Mother of God has been chosen by Him not only to give His Son a human nature, but also to collaborate with the divine Saviour in His work of redemption. Although this idea was but little exploited in the past with a view to proving the bodily Assumption of Mary, it is today found in the first rank. There is a text, Genesis 3, 15, which gives us the principle out of which the Assumption logically will be deduced. In the Bull *Ineffabilis* Pius IX declares that "when it is said 'I will put enmities between thee and the woman, and thy seed and her seed' the Fathers teach that the divine prophecy has clearly and openly indicated the merciful Redeemer of the human race, namely the only Son of God, our Lord, Jesus Christ, and also His blessed Mother, the Virgin Mary, and that it indicates at the same time the very enmities between both of them and the demon. This is why, just as Christ, Mediator between God and men, with His assuming human nature, has erased the decree that was against us by nailing it triumphantly to His Cross, so also the most holy Virgin, who is united to Him by the closest and most indissoluble ties, and who perpetuates in Him and through Him His eternal enmities against the ancient serpent, has in *complete triumph* crushed the head of the poisonous dragon with her immaculate foot." [15]

A constant and unbroken tradition, which was already expressed by St. Justin[16] and which is echoed in the liturgy,[17] has always seen in Mary the "new Eve" who has played a role in our restoration analogous to the one Eve played in our fall. Theologians say, in other terms, that Mary is Christ's companion, His helper, altogether like Him. This takes up a phrase dear to St. Albert the Great, "the Helper of the Redemption." [18] To use a more philosophical formula, Mary is the secondary efficient cause of our redemption, in the sense that she prepares the principal cause and promotes Him in His work.[19] Such is the role that the Gospels and theology assign to Mary, a free collaboration on which God in His unfathomed condescension makes the Incarnation and the Redemption depend.[20] Through her the Son of God receives His Body and Blood, the material of His redemptive sacrifice. Thanks to her, humanity itself cooperates in its own redemption by offering itself to God, through Mary, in union with the divine Victim.[21] For centuries tradition shows Mary to us in this light, according to the expression of Pius IX, "united to Him by the closest and most indissoluble ties." But what the Church affirms further, thanks to a sharpness of vision that surpasses the perspicacity of the most penetrating exegete, is that the role of the new Eve associated with the divine Saviour in His combat as in His victory, *is found to be contained* in Genesis, 3, 15.

Pius IX says that Mary, implicated so intimately in the work of the Saviour, also emerges with a *complete* and *total* victory over the serpent from hell, not indeed alone and independently of her Son, but with Him and through Him. In truth, Mary's victory could not be called complete if she merely escaped the deadly consequences that the serpent had in view by inciting man to disobey God; her victory must contribute its own part, real though secondary, towards annihilating those consequences. In other

83

words, if this victory is to be total it must be both subjective and objective. Now, the consequences at which the demon wished to arrive are the loss of grace, of divine sonship, and the *loss of immortality,* as the threat attached to the transgression, the temptation itself, and the sentence of condemnation insinuate.[22] The Bull *Ineffabilis* is content to emphasize the first victory over sin won by the Immaculate Conception, thanks to a manner of redemption unique in Mary's case. But if this argumentation is valid for the first deadly effect of sin, it has the same force for the second, the loss of immortality. In order to be *completely victorious* over Satan, as Pius IX says, Mary must escape not death itself,[23] but the *kingdom of death* by a resurrection and a corporal Assumption, just as Christ did. St. Paul tells us in I Cor. 15, 20 that in fact as long as the body has not been raised, one may speak of a victory "in hope" but not of one actually won at the present moment. It is in arising that Christ breaks forth into His triumphal hymn, "O death, where is thy victory?" Also for Mary, it is only in arising that she will be completely victorious with Christ and through Him over the demon and over death.

Besides, we see that Mary is forever united with Christ in His work of redemption, which has the negation of sin and its deadly consequences as its purpose. Now this work comprises not only the incarnation and the Passion but also the Resurrection and Christ's definitive triumph in heaven, as the Church

84

gives us to meditate upon in the recitation of the Rosary. If Mary is united to Jesus in His Incarnation and Passion, how will she be separated from Him in His Resurrection and victory? To suppose it, would be to empty Pius IX's magnificent phrase of its full and natural meaning: "She perpetuates in Him and through Him His eternal enmities, and triumphs completely over the serpent."

In a word, in order that the victory won by Mary over Satan and sin may be truly complete and equal to that of the divine Redeemer Himself, it is necessary to acknowledge in Mary not only that dogma of faith which exempts her from concupiscence and which is best symbolized by her perfect virginity, the Immaculate Conception, but also her *bodily Assumption,* which is at present so lucidly proposed by the ordinary magisterium to the belief of the faithful.

The Fathers of the Vatican Council had gone through the argumentation we have just reviewed, and they made it the firm foundation of their postulatum, asking of the infallible Assembly the definition of Mary's bodily Assumption:

"According to the apostolic doctrine expressed in Rom. 5, 8; 1 Cor. 15, 24. 26. 54. 57; Heb. 11, 14. 15; and in other places, the victory of Christ over Satan, the ancient serpent, is made up of a triple victory, as of three integrating parts: victory over sin and its consequences, over concupiscence, and over death. And since Genesis 3, 15 shows the Mother of God as associated in a unique manner with her Son in His

85

triumph, since we are supported by the unanimous vote of the Fathers, *we do not hesitate* to recognize that the foregoing prophecy refers to the Blessed Virgin *in the glory of this triple victory*. Thus, as by her Immaculate Conception she has triumphed over sin, and by her virginal Motherhood over concupiscence, so in fulfillment of the prophecy and following the example of her Son she has won a shining victory over death by her anticipated resurrection." [24]

❖

CHAPTER SIX

Opportuneness of the Definition of the Assumption

THAT the corporal Assumption of Mary can be defined seems to us to be beyond dispute. On the whole, its present state recalls that of the Immaculate Conception about 1850. The grounds for proof in the Bull *Ineffabilis* could be applied point by point to our matter. As for a dogmatic definition, what is it after all but the clear and infallible declaration of what is found to be the Church's traditional faith and the object of the ordinary magisterium's teaching? What the Church today professes in the ordinary way, she can declare without more ado in the extraordinary way to inculcate the revealed truth better, either the better to honor God in His admirable works or to put an end once for all to false opinions and to repress all opposition.

Who can deny that such action is desirable? It is the most ardent desire of all Catholics who have at heart the honor and glory of our Mother in heaven.

After France, which gave birth to an organization of prayer for obtaining from God the favor of a solemn definition of the Assumption, Italy has since 1929 been employed in the same work of propaganda, under the name *Forze Italiane,* with unhoped for success.[1] The Marian congresses, especially that of Nantes, 1924, have labored efficaciously for the same end. We are witnesses to a movement like that which took hold of the Catholic world when the definition of the Immaculate Conception was debated. And since the time when His Holiness Pius XII solemnly consecrated the world to the Immaculate Heart of Mary, an action followed by the Bishops in their own dioceses, this movement that carries souls to Mary to love and glorify her has intensified and broadened.[2]

Who does not desire that an end be put to the hesitations that come to light now and again, even from men who have recognized ability in other lines? These doubts are provoked by the fact that the dogmatic character of the corporal Assumption, its connection with the deposit of faith, is not yet sufficiently accepted by minds too much given to historical criticism. Misled by a care for exclusively historical proofs they come to question, as does J. Ernst,[3] whether the bodily Assumption is a doctrine of faith taught by the Church's ordinary magisterium. They regard it as a pious and probable opinion at the most, which the Church favors without enjoining it. Father Wiederkehr cites the case of a layman otherwise well instructed, who thought on the testimony of a priest that provisionally it was necessary to understand Mary's Assumption solely as the glorification of her soul.[4] Up until the eve of the definition of the Immaculate Conception, men were still met who had not become convinced that this was a truth of our faith. So, as long as the Assumption is not defined, there will still be recalcitrants. A clear and infallible declaration will dissipate all these doubts and put an end to those specious arguments that end by creating uneasiness in men's minds.

But it may be asked whether the time is well chosen for being occupied with a question that needs peace and calm for receiving its final statement. We have just come through the most dreadful war that has been unleashed on humanity; questions of all kinds, international and national, political and social, divide minds without their arriving at any satisfying conclusion. A profound crisis now overturns society and puts in danger traditional ideas and institutions. Numerous ruins still remain unrepaired, and the threat of another possible war weighs on the world always. In these circumstances can one dream of importuning the Holy Father with new postulata for a definition of Mary's bodily Assumption? To stop here would be really to judge the things of God in too human a way. Let us recall with Father Wiederkehr the tragic circumstances in which the finishing touches were put on the dogma of the Immaculate Conception.[5] On November 15, 1848 the Papal minister, Pelligrino Rossi was stabbed and fell dead on the stairs of the Chancellery. Revolution broke out against the Papal government. Assailed by impossible demands, Pius IX took refuge at Gaeta. On February 5, 1849 the Constituent Assembly met, and on the ninth declared the Papal sovereignty abolished. In such a moment of disorder and anguish, on February 2, the Pope addressed himself to all the Bishops of the world to ask of them whether a dogmatic definition of the Immaculate Conception were desired by the clergy and the Christian people. 540 answers decided the Pope to complete the last stage. On December 8, 1854 the official declaration took place at St. Peter's in the presence of 54 Cardinals, 42 Archbishops, 92 Bishops and about 50,000 faithful. It was an act of confidence and courage that was rewarded by remarkable graces.[6] "The definition of the Assumption," writes E. Campana, "will lead humanity back most forcefully to a consideration of our eternal destiny. It will affirm anew and in a special way the dogma of the resurrection of the body, and of the triumph that Christ, the immortal King of ages, has won over sin and its sorrowful effects. The definition would be a shining crown placed on Mary's head by the Church, a crown that would reflect always more light on the grandeur of the faith and of its Author and Finisher, Jesus." [7] A definition of Mary's corporal Assumption in these agitated times in which we live, would be a pledge of grace and peace for souls and for the race, as was the definition of the Immaculate Conception in its own time.

Let us not pass over in silence the important step undertaken by His Holiness Pius XII with a view to defining soon the Assumption.

On May 1, 1946 the Pope addressed himself to the bishops of the whole world, and asked them to show as promptly as possible what they together with the faithful confided to their care thought both of defining the Assumption and of the opportuneness of proclaiming it as a dogma of our faith. This request for enquiry—His Holiness alludes to it himself—recalls the one Pius IX sent out before proclaiming the dogma of the Immaculate Conception. There follows a translation of the document, whose importance can escape no one.

"As the faithful call upon the Virgin Mary, Mother of God, and obtain her constant help, so they endeavor to venerate her always more and more. Now, it is proper to true and deep love that it keeps seeking how to give new signs of affection. Thus the faithful have endeavored throughout the centuries to show and increase this love by an ever growing devotion. We are persuaded that this is why Cardinals, Archbishops and Bishops, religious, associations and universities, a whole multitude of the faithful, have addressed pleas to the Holy See for many years; of which those received between 1848 and 1940 have been gathered into two volumes, edited with com-

91

mentary and recently published. These pleas ask for the proclamation and solemn definition of the Assumption into heaven of the Virgin Mary with her body as a dogma of faith. Surely everyone knows that nearly 200 Bishops of the Vatican Council expressed the same desire with great insistence.

"As for Us, who have been chosen to guard and extend the kingdom of Christ, We have the duty to combat what is harmful and promote what is useful. Thus, since the beginning of our Pontificate, the question We had to set before Ourselves and study is whether it is allowable, opportune and useful that We use Our power to follow up the pleas We mentioned. For this reason We have not omitted, nor do We now omit, to pray with fervor that God may inspire Us and make Us know His most adorable will.

"Unite, Venerable Brethren, your prayers to Ours to obtain this heavenly light. In exhorting you with fatherly care to do so, We are following the example of Our predecessors, and especially of Pius IX regarding the defining of the Immaculate Conception of the Mother of God; and in asking of your good will that you communicate to Us the feeling of the clergy and the faithful committed to your care with respect to the Assumption of the Virgin Mary, We desire most ardently to know if you, Venerable Brethren, in your great wisdom and prudence, think that the corporal Assumption of the holy Virgin can be proposed and defined as a dogma of faith, and if you together with your clergy and people desire it.

"While awaiting your responses—and the sooner they reach Us the more grateful We will be—We ask for you, Venerable Brethren, and for yours the grace of God, and the favor of the generous and august Virgin." [8]

In an audience given to the members of the General Chapter of Servites, His Holiness has already been able to say that the vast majority of the Bishops have given testimony enthusiastically of their own faith in this mystery and of that of their people. He adds that those who raised difficulties against the definition of the Assumption are rare. In a more recent audience, given to the organizers of the Marian Congress on the Assumption of the Congregations of the most Holy Virgin at Barcelona, Pius XII has manifested his intention to proceed without delay to the proclamation of the dogma of the Assumption. Such a promise cannot but bring joy to those who have at heart the glorification of our Mother and Queen.

The Evolution of the Iconography of the Assumption[1]

THE MODE of representing Mary's Assumption has its origin in that of the Lord's Ascension. The Acts of the Apostles uses the words "He was taken up"[2] to describe the last dramatic action in the life of the divine Saviour. The words insinuate that Christ, mounting towards heaven, has been taken, seized, captured by an invisible force which draws Him towards the heights. The Psalmist had already used the same figure to speak of his thanksgiving to God for deliverance from his affliction. "(He) took me: and received me out of many waters."[3] The first artists who have tried to represent the Ascension have translated the text of the Acts with scrupulous realism. A fragment of a sarcophagus at Clermont[4] and an ivory diptych of the fourth century preserved in the Museum of Munich[5] show our Lord scaling the slope of a mountain, while from the clouds there comes forth a hand that takes Him by the arm to lift Him up to the habitation of glory.

94

The first Assumption we know of is presented along similar lines. It adorns the principal side of a fourth century sarcophagus preserved in the Church of Santa Engracia at Saragossa.[6] Framed by more usual scenes from the Gospels: the cure of the man born blind, of the woman with a flow of blood, and the miracle of Cana; there is seen between two persons (Apostles) a woman wrapped in a cloak in an attitude of prayer. The scene recalls almost exactly the figure engraved at the bottom of an ancient gilded chalice. But on the chalice the artist has taken care to designate the persons by name, Mary, St. Peter and St. Paul.[7] On the sarcophagus the person placed on the right of the Virgin is easily recognized as St. Peter. The round head and the curly beard and hair are his traditional features. They are given to us by the small second century bronze disc found by Boldetti in the cemetery of Domitilla where the heads of the two founders of Christian Rome face each other.[8] Also by the two frescos, executed in the third and fourth centuries in the church of Sts. Peter and Marcellinus[9] and in the cemetery of Domitilla.[10] The head of the second Apostle has vanished as a result of mutilation. With Dom Leclercq we can see in this figure on the Spanish sarcophagus a rudimentary Assumption. In any case it seems certain that this is the form under which the first Christian art began to conceive the Virgin's Assumption.

Contrary to this opinion, the Benedictine Father G. Llopart regards the "woman received by God" as a symbol of the city of Saragossa, an interpretation he bases on Clement Prudentius.[11]

1. *Mary "Carried Up" to Heaven*

The Gospel according to St. Luke expresses itself differently from the Acts of the Apostles in relating the Ascension. "Whilst he blessed them, he departed from them, and was carried up to heaven." [12] Syria applies herself to reproducing faithfully in her art St. Luke's expression. On a panel of the door of St. Sabina at Rome, where Syrian influence is undeniable, the new image seems to have its origin. Christ, in the presence of only four Apostles, is almost snatched away from the earth by two powerful angels who lean towards Him and grasp Him by the arms.[13] Soon Christ appears to us soaring above the Apostles *carried by angels*. A miniature in the Rabula manuscript[14] and some ampullas from Monza, the gift of Pope Gregory the Great to the queen Theodolinda,[15] show Christ seated or standing and enveloped completely by the outline of an immense halo, a kind of rigid frame which the angels hold up in their hands and carry towards heaven, while below the Apostles, stunned and saddened, look on the Master Who is leaving them. Mary's Assumption borrows its essential features from this representation. The Virgin, however, keeps her ancient attitude of prayer. Further, a text from the pseudo-Mileto encourages the artists to show Mary rising to heaven and *carried by angels*. At the end of the narrative the divine Master

96

repeats His promise to the Apostles to remain with them forever, before leaving them. "And immediately," the text continues, "the Lord was raised up into a cloud and was received into heaven, and *the angels with Him, carrying the blessed Mary into the paradise of God.*" [16] This is the form under which Mary is shown on the embroidered cloth of the seventh or eighth century preserved in the Cathedral of Sens. In broad elliptical medallions, placed side by side, Mary in prayer is seen to soar above the ten Apostles who hold a cross in their right hand. She is attended by two angels who with one hand hold up a palm of triumph and with the other seem to sustain the flight of the risen Mother.[17] Without doubt it is under this form also that the faithful could already contemplate on feast days the Assumption pictured on the precious vestments offered to the Church of St. Mary Major by the Popes Hadrian I [18] and Pascal I.[19] At any rate, we still possess an ivory of St. Gall, of perhaps the eighth or ninth century, where Mary in prayer is accompanied by four angels who with raised hands gaze upon and admire her. Here the Apostles are absent. But that the image may be well understood, the artist has carved above it in the frame the words: "The Ascension of the Holy Mary." [20]

The Syrian formula of the Assumption will allow the German miniaturists of the eleventh and twelfth centuries to transform the Falling Asleep itself, which was bequeathed by Byzantium to the West. Byzantine art, which seems to have ignored the Assumption properly so called, was content to represent the Falling Asleep. Both fresco and mosaic lay Mary out upon her funeral bed among the Apostles miraculously assembled around her. Christ Himself is standing in the center of the scene. He welcomes the soul of His Mother under the form of a child, and commits it to the two angels that accompany Him to carry it to the dwelling of beatitude. All these details are taken from the Apocrypha. After having given His commands to the Apostles for the burial of Mary, "the Lord," according to the pseudo-Mileto, "gave the soul of our holy Mother Mary to His Archangel Michael, the overseer of Paradise and the leader of the Hebrew people, and Gabriel the Archangel went along with it." [21] John of Thessalonica repeats in his turn that "the Lord upon receiving her soul confided it to the care of Michael, after He had wrapped it in veils of shining splendor." [22] During the Ottonian epoch, about the tenth century, numerous ivories render the subject popular in Germany.[23] The German miniaturists made themselves masters of this mode in their turn, but they transformed it slightly and made it a representation of the Assumption. In a minature of the eleventh century Gospel Book of Bertold, preserved at Salzburg, the child that the divine Master hands to the angel is no longer a baby wrapped in veils but on a small scale the exact replica of the Virgin whom four Apostles are laying in the sarcophagus.[24] To dispel all uncertainty a

Book of Collects of Hildesheim from the eleventh century breaks the scene into parts. In one miniature Christ presents to two angels the soul of Mary pictured in the usual guise of a small child; in another the same angels carry to heaven a frame in which Mary is seen from head to waist, while from above the hand of God stretches out of heaven to welcome the risen virgin.[25] Thus the German miniaturists hold to the Syrian form of the Assumption and complete in a naive manner the scene of the Falling Asleep. Other eleventh century miniaturists show the glorified Virgin either from head to waist or fully, *enclosed in a round or oval nimbus* which the angels hold and carry towards heaven.[26]

When they read the Apocrypha themselves, the artists of the West will soon imagine a new Assumption. The great happening will no longer unfold in the death-room of the Virgin, but in the Valley of Josaphat close to her tomb. A variant in the Coptic narrative of the Assumption tells that on August 15 the divine Master again appeared to His disciples who were gathered around the tomb of the Virgin, and told them that the soul of Mary was about to descend from heaven. It goes on: "We looked right in front of us, and behold! we saw a great chariot of light drawn by Cherubim, and in it the holy Virgin Mary was seated shining brighter than the sun and the moon . . . At the call of the Lord the body of the Virgin, His Mother, arose from the tomb. He infused her soul again into her body and we saw her

99

living as before. *And our Lord stretched out His hand* and placed her with Him in the chariot of glory." [27] The pseudo-Mileto keeps to essentially the same story. When the Apostles had buried the body of Mary in the Valley of Josaphat, Jesus appeared to them again. In the name of all the others Peter prayed the Lord to raise His Mother and to take her with Him to heaven. "Then the Lord said: Let your desire be fulfilled! And He commanded the Archangel Michael to fetch the holy soul of Mary. And soon, when the Archangel Gabriel had taken away the stone from the entrance to the tomb, the Lord said, 'Arise, My beloved, My nearest of kin. Since you have not felt the disorder of the flesh by contact with man, you shall not suffer the body's corruption in the grave.' And at once Mary arose . . . and after He had embraced her, the Lord gave her to the angels to escort her into Paradise." [28]

In the tympanum above the left door of the west facade of Notre Dame in Paris, the door of the Virgin, the sculptor has reproduced the legendary story with admirable art. Our Lord has just descended among the Apostles gathered around the Virgin's tomb. With the tranquillity of omnipotence He touches Mary's extended body with His left hand, while the right is raised in a gesture of benediction. From his partly open mouth have just sprung the words, "Arise My beloved, My nearest of kin." Obeying the invitation of her Son, Mary raises herself from the tomb. Gracious and smiling she awakes from sleep and joins her hands in a gesture of adoration and recognition. The two angels, St. Michael and St. Gabriel, who are placed at the head and foot of the sarcophagus, prepare with a movement both spontaneous and graceful to carry her away decorously in the very cloth that served for her shroud.[29] A few years before at Senlis another sculptor had been content to represent the angels crowding in nimble flight around Mary resurrected to carry her to the abode of happiness. Nothing is more exquisite than these smiling angels, almost immaterial under the narrow folds of their tunics. "All lean forward, attentive and joyous, living and charming with feeling and poetry." [30] An Italian painter of the fourteenth century, Taddeo di Bartolo, has also sought to fix with his brush the moment when Christ raises His Mother. Carried on the wings of angels, the divine Master comes down towards the tomb and stretches His hand towards Mary asleep in death. At this touch Mary raises herself above the coffin, ready to take flight.

In the sculpture of Notre Dame of Paris we do not see the Apostles scrutinize anxiously the empty tomb. A different apocryphal story, which we saw was born towards the end of the tenth or the beginning of the eleventh century,[31] is going to suggest this new attitude to the artists. It is the famous Euthymiac legend, or the legend of St. Thomas. The legend tells that St. Thomas, since he had arrived after Mary's burial, had the tomb opened for himself. It was found empty, or containing no more than the funeral clothes, roses and lilies. Later, towards the beginning of the thirteenth century, an unpublished episode[32] is attached to this account. It tells that the risen Virgin had left her cincture in the hands of St. Thomas. But there are some differences regarding the interpretation of this act. Some—such as Jacopo de Voragine, the author of the Golden Legend—see in it a sensible sign for the purpose of vanquishing the incredulity of the recalcitrant Apostle; others—and this is the version which especially made way in Italy —see in the cincture a pledge granted by Mary to the Apostle so he could convince the other Apostles of the truth of the Virgin's resurrection and Assumption, which he himself had looked on from the heights of the Mount of Olives. The city of Prato boasts possession of this precious cincture. They tell that a young man named Michele dei Dagomari brought it from Jerusalem in 1141 on his return from the first Crusade. He had found it, they add, in the house of a Greek priest whose daughter he sought in marriage. In 1312 an attempt at robbery, which almost succeeded, determined the city to build a special sanctuary beside the cathedral to protect the relic from all danger of theft.

A disciple of Giotto, Agnolo Gaddi, was commissioned about 1365 to decorate the famous Chapel of the Cincture with frescos, and he is without doubt one of the first to reproduce the episode.[33] In the Botticelli painting preserved at Florence in the Uffizi gallery, we are made to assist at the unfolding of the whole drama. While Thomas contemplates the flight of the Virgin on the Mount of Olives, and sees himself favored by her with the cincture, in the foreground the Apostles stare into the empty tomb. The most beautiful work, however, that this episode has inspired is that of Sodoma, the disciple of Leonardo da Vinci, in the Oratory of St. Bernardine at Sienna. Before the eyes of the enraptured Apostles Mary arises from the sarcophagus filled to overflowing with roses and lilies. She is enthroned now on a rock-like cloud. She has undone her cincture, and with a gesture of exquisite kindness, that is emphasized by her look, her smile and her right hand extended to protect and bless, she lets the long flowing band slip from her left hand, while the kneeling Apostle, happy and amazed, receives it in his hands.[34] Even when the painters have St. Thomas mingle with the other Apostles around the tomb of the Virgin, they sometimes place the cincture in his hands as a kind of identifying badge. Thus he appears in the resurrection of the Virgin by Taddeo di Bartolo, and in the coronation of Mary by Raphael.[35]

Preoccupied solely with looking at and inspecting the empty tomb the Apostles seem for a long time not to perceive the prodigy that is unfolding above their heads. The inspection of the tomb and the resurrection of the Virgin are separated into two sections, even in the same picture, and are not only separated but separate. We see this division in the picture of

Taddeo di Bartolo and in Bartolomeo della Gatta's. Little by little, however, the Apostles raise their heads and begin to join in the glory of their queen. Without taking an active part in the drama which is played above them, they guess it and begin to glimpse it. The works of Pinturicchio, of Raphael, of his disciple Jules Romain and of Dürer[36] reflect this intermediary stage that prepares for the master-piece of Titian.

While the Apostles examine the tomb and are associated little by little with the miracle which their Mother and Queen enjoys, Mary rises towards glory in the fulness of life she has gained. In picturing this ascension the artists are always inspired by the ancient Syrian tradition bequeathed to them by the miniaturists. Whether seated or standing, Mary remains enclosed in a rigid almond-shaped halo which the angels carry to heaven. The Siennese Simone Memmi, Lippo Memmi, Pietro Lorenzetti; the sculptors Andrea Orcagna,[37] Mino da Fiesole, and down to the della Robbias always keep to the old form. On the exterior walls of the apse of Notre Dame in Paris,[38] on the door of the Mandorla of the Basilica in Florence,[39] on the great door of the Cathedral of Magdeburg,[40] the same is true.

A frame so rigid, however, could not satisfy an esthetic feeling more in love with beauty, grace and harmony. Accordingly, we see this geometric outline give place more and more to a living nimbus.

Masolino, at the beginning of the fifteenth century imagines a double row of angels around the Virgin; Perugino, Pinturicchio and Matteo Balducci frame the risen Virgin in an oval nimbus formed of two parallel lines between which appear the heads of small angels. At the end of the fifteenth century, on the eve of the height of the Renascence, the artists remain thus enslaved to the ancient formula. A long time before, however, the genius of Donatello had inaugurated a new theme and outlined the way of the future on the front of Cardinal Brancacci's sarcophagus. Around the Virgin he had sculptured living angels in impetuous flight, graced with a strong and supple motion. They dip, they soar, they glide into the clouds, raising the Mother up to the throne of her Son. The Virgin, seated, is admirable, grave and sad. She does not forget the poor banished children of Eve who sigh and weep in this valley of tears, and with hands joined in a gesture of tenderness and supplication she seems already to be interceding for them. She is the Dolorosa even in her triumph.[41]

We see that Donatello keeps an essential element of the old formula even though he breaks through it. *Mary is carried* by strong and powerful angels. This idea will be maintained for a long time to come. Even the Baroque period will be slow to forsake it. Guido Reni, Nicolas Poussin[42] and even Rubens, in several of their Assumptions, will remember the ancient tradition. Well into the nineteenth century Pierre Proud'hon will picture two powerful angels carrying Mary to the habitation of glory.[43]

2. Mary "Mounting" into Heaven

Theology, however, has affirmed unwaveringly since the Middle Ages that the Virgin was gifted with a marvelous agility, and that she had no need of other help in order to rise into heaven. Sodoma understands that the theological thought could be also the most esthetic. In his picture in the oratory of St. Bernardine, of which we have spoken above, the great pupil of Leonardo da Vinci places the Virgin in a nimbus of small mirthful angels who gambol among the clouds and crowd around their Queen.

We find all these advances, the fruit of groping but tenacious and continued effort, in that magnificent symphony where all is harmony, order and beauty: the Assunta of Titian. The great Venetian painter has borrowed from Correggio the glistening splendor of colors and the exuberance of life that is reflected in glorified bodies, and from Luini and Gaudenzio Ferrari the gathering and concentration of feeling. Never had such luminous radiance sprung from the Venetian palette. The Apostles, harmoniously grouped, tend with all their being towards their Mother, impatient to follow her uprising as though raised up by an irresistible desire, while they stand shrouded in the shadow that forever bathes a world subject to suffering despite its flashes of vision through faith. And in a nimbus of agile and graceful little angels, her feet set lightly on vaporous, insubstantial clouds, as though raised up by a strong and mysterious breeze that spreads wide her mantle of purple, her face shining with happiness and her eyes filled with ecstasy, Mary *lifts herself* towards an ocean of light, in the full maturity of her grace and beauty. And already above, God the Father, shown with marvelous foreshortening, all smiles and welcomes, opens His arms lovingly and makes ready to welcome His privileged creature. The angel who accompanies Him, one of the most beautiful creations of the great Venetian painter, turns his eyes towards God, eyes quivering, as it were, with a repressed eagerness, and he awaits from Him the signal that will at last let him place on Mary's head the royal diadem he carries in his hands.[44] No artist has ever reproduced better the fulness of human happiness, alas! too uniquely human. To transform this overflowing voluptuousness into a more subtle spiritual ecstasy Titian needs the soul of Fra Angelico. Such as it is, however, the work merited the enthusiasm with which it was welcomed by the whole city of Venice. Artists will come to admire it and to profit by it. For Guido Reni, Paolo Veronese, Rubens himself and van Loon, Titian remains the master.

Titian does not, however, cause us to forget Correggio. Between 1525 and 1530 Antonio Allegri had undertaken to decorate the cupola of the Cathedral of Parma. With an enchanting art, that one would wish less sensual and naturalistic, he had painted there the flight of the Virgin towards the dizzying heights of heaven. Openly criticized by some, admired by others,[45] the work impressed all. It is from Correggio above all that the Baroque artists are going to learn the art of giving to Mary as she rises to heaven an irresistible transport. Domenichino in the church of Santa Maria in Trastevere, Pozzi in St. Ignatius will reveal that they are disciples of Correggio. In the picture of Annibal Carrache the Virgin with ecstatic face and eyes fixed on heaven lifts herself above the tomb with the magnificent surge of a great bird taking flight. Radiant, she arises towards the light. Guido Reni in Italy, Pacheco in Spain, Philippe de Champaigne in France, and above all Rubens, the sumptuous painter who will undertake to paint the Assumption a dozen times without repeating himself,[46] continue in their own manner the grand art of Correggio.

In order to give a still more perfect delineation of the Assumption, however, it was necessary to disengage it further from every earthly tie and from every savor of the Apocrypha. Since Giotto religious art had begun to mingle later personages in the Gospel scenes. From this time St. Francis is seen kneeling on Golgotha, contemplating the Crucified. In the fifteenth century this attempt at actualization becomes more and more generalized. The artists took up the habit of mixing other saints, bishops, virgins or martyrs, with the Apostles, the witnesses of the Assumption. Not content to be joined with the Apostles the other saints sometimes substitute for them. The historical delineation is thus changed into a spiritual and mystic one. Botticelli groups four saints around the Virgin crowned in glory: an Apostle, a cardinal and two bishops. Fra Angelico and Pietro del Pollaiuolo were before him in this. The grand vision that had thrown the Apostles into astonishment and that shone in the souls of the saints and faithful, must at length cause the framework given in the Apocrypha to be forgotten, and even cause the witnesses of the drama to vanish. It is this vision, freed from every earthly tie and from every reminder of the Apocrypha, that art aspired to represent through painting and sculpture. This is the theme that Donatello was among the first, if not the first, to deal with on one of the sides of Cardinal Brancacci's sarcophagus.[47] Titian took it up at Venice in his fresco for the Chapel of St. Zeno in the Church of the Crusaders. Mary, surrounded by angels and with arms extended and eyes opened widely on the Uncreated Glory, rises towards God in irresistible flight. Guido Reni, Pacheco, Nicolas Poussin and Philippe de Champaigne will do nothing more than exploit the master idea of the Venetian painter in their own manner. What we always see is Mary, either borne up by angels or lifting herself with spontaneous motion, but freed from every reminder of earth, mounting upwards in the serenity of space.

109

We have met with two formulas at the beginnings of the representation of the Assumption, one western, the other Syrian. The first is free from any influence of the Apocrypha, the second is inspired by it. But *in their expression* both of them, it seems, are linked up with the two descriptions of our Lord's ascension suggested by the words of the Acts and the Gospel according to St. Luke.

The western formula would scarcely favor a true work of art that could satisfy both esthetics and piety. One lasting element, however, ought to be noted. For a long time the Virgin keeps her attitude of prayer. Sometimes also in the Ottonian miniatures we see the hand of God come forth from heaven to welcome or crown Mary. But important as these details may be, the formula itself did not develop. It remained sterile. On the other hand a long life was reserved for the Syrian conception. We have seen it assert itself from the seventh or eighth century, and without doubt we ought to deplore the disappearance of other works. To it the miniaturists of the eleventh and twelfth recur, though awkwardly, to transform the Byzantine Falling Asleep into an Assumption.

The awakening of the Virgin sleeping in death, the scrutiny of the tomb emptied of its treasure, the cincture of the Virgin bestowed upon the Apostle Thomas as a proof or pledge of the resurrection and assumption of the Mother of God, are three western episodes which through the art of the Middle Ages recall the apocryphal narratives. They do not modify, however, the representation of the Assumption itself: Mary enclosed in an immense almond-shaped nimbus, as in a rigid frame, remains always entrusted to the angels charged with carrying her to heaven. Artistic sense, as well as theological ideas, will cause this crude enclosure to disappear gradually, and will create for the glorified Mother of God that charming retinue of little angels who are bathed in her glory. The work of Titian collects and orchestrates the successive gains. Baroque art, working according to the spirit by which it lives, will set itself to impress on Mary as she mounts to heaven a flight more spontaneous, more vehement, more dizzying.

Finally, leaving aside the frame inside which the Assumption unfolds, for it is still too heavy, religious art creates a purified representation—as it had done for the Immaculate Conception—in which we see only Mary, in the splendor of refound life and transfigured by glory, mount towards the throne of God with the escort of angels, or carried by them, there to be crowned Queen and Sovereign of the world.

Notes

❖

NOTES TO INTRODUCTION

[1] P. Renaudin, *La doctrine de l'Assomption de la Très Sainte Vierge, sa définibilité comme dogme de foi,* Paris, 1913.

[2] G. Mattiussi, *L'Assunzione corporea della Vergine Madre di Dio,* Milan, 1924.

[3] F. X. Godts, *Définibilité dogmatique de l'Assomption corporelle de la Sainte Vierge,* Esschen, 1924.

[4] V. Bainvel, "La définibilité de l'Assomption," *Congrès marial de Nantes,* 1925, p. 144.

[5] J. Ernst, *Die leibliche Himmelfahrt Mariä,* Regensburg, 1921.

[6] *op. cit.,* pp. 5, 43, 64.

[7] *Lintzer . . . Quartalschrift,* t. 74 (1921), pp. 226-237, 381-389; t. 77 (1924), pp. 449-455; t. 78 (1925), pp. 34-45, 260-273; t. 80 (1927), pp. 532-544.

[8] J. Ernst, "Neues zur Knotroverse über die Definierbarkeit der Himmelfahrt Mariä," *Bonner Zeitschrift,* t. 6 (1929), pp. 289-304; t. 7 (1930), pp. 16-31.

[9] P. Wiederkehr, *Die leibliche Aufnahme der allerseligsten Jungfrau Mariä in den Himmel,* Einsiedeln, 1927.

[10] Aug. Deneffe, "Gehört die Himmelfahrt Mariä zum Galubensschatz?" *Scholastik,* t. III (1928), pp. 190-218.

Cf. Jean Rivière, "Chronique de theologie dogmatique," *Revue des Sciences Religieuses*, t. xii (1932), pp. 82-86.

[11] Fr. Müller, *Origo divino-apostolica evectionis Beatissimae Virginis ad gloriam caelestem quoad corpus,* Innsbruck, 1930. Cf. J. Rivière, *op. cit.*, pp. 87-88.

[12] J. Rivière, *op. cit.*, p. 86.

[13] *op. cit.*, p. 89.

NOTES TO CHAPTER ONE

[1] Cf. St. Thomas, *Summa,* 1, 1, 6 ad 3; 1, 1, 7 & 8; 1 2, 111, 4. Also L. de Grandmaison, *Le dogme chrétien,* Paris, 1928, pp. 251s.

[2] Pohle, *Lehrbuch der Dogmatik,* 4th edition, Paderborn, 1909, t. ii, p. 294.

[3] Cf. Denzinger, *Enchiridion,* nos. 256 & 993.

[4] This message is to be "faithfully kept and infallibly declared as the divine deposit of Christ, the Spouse, handed down" (to us). Vatican Council. Cf. Denzinger, no. 1800.

[5] de Grandmaison, *op. cit.*, p. 183.

[6] [This needs explanation. Strictly speaking, Christian revelation closed with the death of the last Apostle. Cf. Denzinger, nos. 783 & 2021. *Trans. note.*]

[7] John 14, 25s.

[8] This is verified likewise in the case of Mary's corporal Assumption, which we will see is virtually included in the virginal Motherhood of Mary such as God wished it to be in fact.

[9] de Grandmaison, *op. cit.*, pp. 182-225.

[10] *ibid.*, pp. 226-274.

[11] *ibid.*, p. 256.

114

[12] *ibid.*, pp. 263s.

[13] Ephesians 4, 13.

[14] de Grandmaison, *op. cit.*, pp. 262s.

[15] *ibid.*, pp. 266-270.

[16] *ibid.*, p. 274.

[17] John 17, 3.

[18] Colossians 1, 20.

[19] Ephesians 1, 9s.

[20] Colossians 1, 20; Ephesians 1, 7; Galatians 4, 4ss.

[21] "And him (God) gave as head over all the Church, which indeed is his body, the fulness of him who is wholly fulfilled in all." Ephesians 1, 22s.

[22] St. Augustine, *De Agone*, c. 24, PL., 40, 303.

[23] "The Church defines as a necessary object of explicit belief only what she sees through the assistance of the Holy Spirit to be virtually contained in a formally revealed object of faith." de Grandmaison, *op. cit.*, p. 262. There exist other truths in Holy Scripture which have only an accidental and extrinsic connection with the message of our salvation. Scripture relates, for example, that Timothy had a weak stomach, that St. Paul had left his cloak at Troas, and other similar facts. These facts come under divine faith, because they are revealed, but they will never become dogmas. Besides these truths, said to be revealed extrinsically and non-essentially, there are others that have a more intimate bond with revealed truths. These are, among others, philosophical truths which revealed truths imply or suppose. They are said to be intrinsically revealed, though not essentially so. It happens that the Church defines them as she defined in the council of Vienne, under pain of heresy, that the soul is the form of the body. (Cf. Denzinger, nos. 480 & 738.) Perhaps it would be better, in this case, to speak of an

115

infallible decision rather than a solemn dogmatic definition.

24 [Since Elias appeared with Christ at the Transfiguration, and Christ Himself said, "Elias indeed is to come and will restore all things" (Matthew 17, 3 & 11), it seems premature to suggest that Elias or his state has no "close connection with the essential doctrine of our salvation." *Trans. note.*]

25 K. Wiederkehr, *Die leibliche Aufnahme der allerseligsten Jungfrau Maria in den Himmel,* Einsiedeln, 1927, pp. 52-55.

26 Psalm 2, 8; 21, 19.

27 Matthew 28, 19ss.

28 Acts 11, 20ss.

29 Acts 10, 48.

30 Denzinger, no. 1100.

31 Cf. V. Bainvel, *De Magisterio vivo et Traditione,* Paris. 1905, pp. 103ss. and Vacant, *Le Magistère ordinaire,* Paris, 1887.

32 "It belongs to an Ecumenical Council and the Roman Pontiff speaking *ex cathedra* to pronounce judgments of this kind." *Codex juris canonici,* 1323 #1.

33 *ibid.* Cf. also Vatican Council, Denzinger, no. 1792; cf. also no. 1683.

34 *ibid.,* 1322 #1. Cf. also Denzinger 1797, 1798 & 1800; John 14, 26; 1 Timothy 1, 15.

35 Cf. V. Bainvel, *De Magisterio vivo . . . ,* p. 104.

36 *ibid.,* p. 94ss. Also P. de la Barre, *Vie du dogme,* part ii, c. 2. It is useful to recall here Melchior Cano's principle: If there is anything approved of in the Church by the common agreement of the faithful, a thing which human power indeed could not bring about, then it is necessarily

derived from the tradition of the Apostles. Cano, *De locis theologicis,* 1. III, c. 4; vid. also 1. IV, c. 6 ad 14.

[37] *ibid.,* pp. 82-89.

[38] "Not only external observance but also an internal religious assent of the mind—not firm indeed and absolute, but proportioned to the authority of the decree—must be given to decrees that are not infallible, as long as the contrary is not evident." Bainvel, *De Magisterio* . . . , p. 106. Cf. also *Codex.* 1323 #1.

[39] Denzinger, no. 1683.

[40] *Summa,* 2 2, 53, 3 ad 2. "(If something is done) out of contempt for the ruling norm, this properly is implied by rashness."

[41] "For such a definition it is sufficient that some supernatural truth be contained implicitly in Tradition or Scripture, so that with the increasingly common agreement of the Church, the Church herself can express her definition, which has for us the force of revelation on account of the infallible assistance of the Holy Spirit." Suarez, *Disputationes in III partem divi Thomae,* q. 27, a. 1, disp. 3, sec. 6, no. 4.

[42] The exposition we have just given of the theological principles that govern the development of dogma and the belief of the faithful, allows us to judge how far Dr. Ernst has gone astray when he writes at the beginning of his little book on the corporal Assumption of Mary: "Without speaking of Holy Scripture at this moment, ecclesiastical Tradition is insufficient regarding Mary's bodily Assumption into heaven. From the point of view of time and space it is neither universal nor continuous; it cannot be followed back to the beginning of Christianity; it is not sufficiently authentic. Consequently, so far from guaran-

teeing for us that the bodily Assumption is part of the deposit of faith, it does not even establish that the Assumption, in its general effect, is a certain fact." (Ernst, *Die leibliche Himmelfahrt Mariä,* p. 10.) In these assertions, which rule the whole thesis of the author, there is clearly a confusion between scientific tradition and dogmatic tradition. If dogmatic tradition must have its foundation in a scientific tradition, neither the virginity of Mary nor especially her Immaculate Conception could ever have been defined. Dr. Ernst seems not to recognize that dogmatic tradition evolves on a plane altogether different from that of historical science and even of theological science. Only the Church holds the deposit of faith and reveals to us its hidden treasures under the impulse of the Holy Spirit and the needs of the moment. Again, in order that a dogmatic truth may be imposed on our faith under pain of rashness, it suffices that the Church by her ordinary magisterium teach it to the faithful by attaching it to the deposit of faith *at any given moment, even after centuries of apparent silence.* And the mere fact that the Church proposes a truth for our belief guarantees for us, better than any historical proof whatsoever, that it is contained in the Apostolic revelation, at least in germ. So, if one wished to know whether the bodily Assumption of Mary makes up part of this primitive revelation and whether, at the same time, it is capable of dogmatic definition, it is sufficient to ask whether *now* the Church teaches it to the Christian world as a truth to be believed by her ordinary magisterium. As Father d'Alès has written so well regarding Dr. Ernst's endeavor, this "argumentation is out of line as regards its leading point of view because it fails to recognize a much more considerable fact: the sense of the Christian people—I would much rather say the sense of the Church—to whom God has given to contemplate in increasing brightness the connection between the privilege of the Assumption and all of God's conduct towards the glorious Virgin. One ought not close one's eyes to this increasing light. To reëstablish the exegesis of an ancient text is always opportune. But the living consciousness of the Christian people, supported by the universal Church's law of prayer, has a quite different authority for establishing the law of belief." Cf. "Bulletin de théologie historique," *Recherches des Sciences Religieuses*, t. xv (1925), p. 579.

NOTES TO CHAPTER TWO

[1] Scheeben, *Handbuch d. Dogmatik*, t. iii, p. 572.

[2] Pohle, *Lehrbuch d. Dogmatik*, t. ii (1909), p. 293.

[3] Jugie, "La Mort et l'Assomption de la Sainte Vierge dans la Tradition des cinq premiers siècles," *Echos d'Orient*, 1926 & 1927.

[4] Cf. Cavallera, "A propos d'une enquête patristique sur l'Assomption," *Bulletin de littérature ecclésiastique*, 1926, p. 97. Also, Rivière, "Questions mariales d'actualité," *Revue des sciences Religieuses*, t. xii (1932), pp. 78-81. In his great work published at Rome in 1944, "*La Mort et l'Assomption de la Sainte Vierge*, étude historico-doctrinale," Father Jugie had taken account of these critics and has given up basing belief in the Assumption on history. But as far as we can see, it is impossible to follow the author further when he tries to derive the Assumption from the dogma of the Immaculate Conception. Our work, conceived on another plane, does not allow us to give a detailed criticism at the moment of the

work of the eminent orientalist, otherwise so richly documented. A sketch of its main outlines will be found in Father Charles Balic's article "De definibilitate assumptionis B. Virginis in caelum," *Antonianum*, t. xxi (1926), pp. 3-67.

[5] Rivière, *loc. cit.*, p. 81.

[6] H. Leclercq, *Dictionnaire d'Archéologie et de Liturgie chrétiennes*, t. i, col. 2991, fig. 1026.

[7] Benedict xiv, *De Festis M. Virginis*, part ii, c. 117.

[8] J. Jürgens, "Kirchliche Ueberlieferung von der leiblichen Aufnahme Maria's in den Himmel," *Zeitschr. für kath. Theologie*, t. iv (1880), pp. 604-606.

[9] Wiederkehr, *Die leibliche Aufnahme der allerseligsten Jungfrau Maria in den Himmel*, Einsiedeln, 1927, pp. 15-26.

[10] Ernst, *Die leibliche Himmelfahrt Mariä*, pp. 10-11.

[11] *Advers. Haeres*, 78, 11; PG, 42, 715. Also 78, 24; PG, 42, 738.

[12] G. Bardy, art. "Ascètes," *Dictionnaire de droit canon*, t. i, col. 1080.

[13] *Advers. Haeres.*, 78, 24; PG, 42, 738.

[14] Apocalypse 12, 13.

[15] *Advers. Haeres.*, 78, 11; PG, 42, 715.

[16] On the Collyridians of Arabia see the important article of Franz Dölger, "Die eigenartige Marienverehung der Philomarianiten oder Kollyridianer in Arabien," *Antike und Christentum*, t. i (1929), pp. 107-142.

[17] *Advers. Haeres.* 78, 24; PG, 42, 738 & 78, 11; PG 42, 715.

[18] *ibid.*, 78, 24; PG 42, 737.

[19] According to the mind of St. Epiphanius there seems to be no doubt that the idolatrous cult of the Collyridians was at least partly based on belief in Mary's immortality.

They were convinced that Mary enjoyed glory without end both in body and soul. This belief must have existed in certain Christian centers before it degenerated into abuse. St. Epiphanius does not deny it. He tries merely to keep it within proper limits.

[20] Ernst, "Neues zur Kontroverse über die Definierbarkeit der Himmelfahrt Mariä," *Bonner Zeitschr. f. Theologie und Seelsorge,* t. vi (1929), p. 292, note 11.

[21] Luke 1, 42.

[22] Luke 1, 48. Note St. Epiphanius's expression "in blessings" and the verb "will bless me" in the Magnificat.

[23] *Advers. Haeres.* 78, 24 (PG 42, 738).

[24] Lipsius, *Die Apokryphe Apostelgeschichte,* t. i (1883), p. 445, note 1 & p. 500. Also H. Delehaye, *Commentarius perpetuus in Martyrologium Hieronymianum ad recensionem H. Quentin,* Brussels, 1931, ad. vi Kal. Jan. (December 27)

[25] *Adver. Haeres.* 79, 5 (PG 42, 748).

[26] *ibid.,* 79, 5 (PG 42, 747).

[27] *ibid.,* 78, 11 (PG 42, 715); 79, 9 (PG 42, 714).

[28] H. Usener, *Der hl. Theodosius,* Leipzig, 1890, pp. 38 & 144.

[29] Fr. Dölger, in *Antike und Christentum,* t. i (1929), p. 141. For the feast of the Virgin celebrated in Palestine in the fifth century consult B. Capelle, "La fête de la Vierge à Jerusalem au Vme siècle," *Le Muséon,* t. 56 (1943), pp. 1-33.

[30] Cf. F. C. Conybeare, *Rituale Armenorum,* Oxford, 1905.

[31] Cf. G. Klameth, *Die neutestamentlichen Lokaltraditionen Palestinas,* Münster, 1914, pp. 60-71.

[32] Cf. E. Schwartz, *Kyrillos von Skythopolis,* TU, 49, 2, Leipzig, p. 236.

[33] G. M. Roschini, *Mariologia,* t. III, Rome, 1948, p. 150.

[34] Cf. PO, 19, 336-343.

[35] Cf. *Homily 67* (PO, 8, 349ff).

[36] On the Syrian influence in Merovingian Gaul cf. L. Bréhier and L. Jalabert, *Byzantin. Zeitschrift,* t. XII (1903); *Revue de l'Orient chrétien,* t. XII (1904); *Dictionnaire d'Archéologie et de Liturgie chrét.,* art. "Colonies," t. II, col. 266; *Histoire du Moyen Age,* (coll. Glotz, t. I, "Des destinées de l'Empire en Occident, de 395-888") Paris, 1928, p. 354.

[37] Cf. PL, 71, 713.

[38] Cf. A. Raes, "Aux origines de la fête de l'Assomption," *Orientalia christiana periodica,* t. XII (1946), 264-266.

[39] Cf. "Brevarium de Jérusalem" and "L'Anonyme de Plaisance," CSEL, t. 39, 155 & 170.

[40] Cf. Jugie, *La mort et l'Assomption de la sainte Vierge,* p. 218.

[41] Cf. PO, t. 19, 376.

[42] Cf. PG, 86, 3280B.

[43] *ibid.,* 86, 3296C.

[44] *ibid.,* 86, 3281C.

[45] *ibid.,* 86, 3312A.

[46] *ibid.,* 86, 3296; see a similar idea developed by Chrysippus of Jerusalem, PO, t. 19, 340-341.

[47] *ibid.,* 86, 3312B&C.

[48] Nicephorus Callistus, *Historia Ecclesiastica,* XVII, 82 (PG, 147, 292).

[49] Cf. A. Raes, *op. cit.,* pp. 269-272.

[50] *ibid.,* p. 273.

[51] M. R. James, *The Apocryphal New Testament,* Oxford, 1924, p. 199.

[52] *ibid.,* p. 197.

[53] Dom Capelle, "La Fête de l'Assomption," *Ephemerides theol. lovan.*, t. III (1926), 38.

[54] Cf. Dom Capelle, "Les anciens récits de l'Assomption et Jean de Thessalonique," *Recherches de théologie ancienne et médiévale*, t. XII (1940), 209-235.

[55] Cf. PG, 86, 3278.

[56] Cf. *Echos d'Orient*, t. XXV (1922), 293-305; t. XXVI (1923), 385-397.

[57] Capelle, *op. cit.*, p. 34.

[58] Cf. A. Baumstark, *Liturgie comparée*, p. 203.

[59] Scheeben, *Dogmatik*, t. III, 585.

[60] *loc. cit.;* see also B. H. Merkelbach, *Mariologia*, Paris, 1939, p. 279.

[61] Ernst, *Die leibliche Himmelfahrt Mariä*, p. 40; see also pp. 35-43.

[62] Cf. Dölger in *Antike und Christentum*, t. I (1929), p. 141.

[63] PG, 97, 1072; cf. also 1088 & 1104.

[64] The doubt regarding Mary's resurrection comes to light even in one of the most ancient apocryphal narratives. It is attributed to St. Cyril of Jerusalem, and ends thus: "A sweet perfume was emitted from the place where the Virgin's body had lain and a voice was heard, 'Take no trouble to look for it until the day of Christ's appearance.'" (Cf. M. R. James, *op. cit.*, pp. 197-198.) A further graeco-syriaco-arabian retouching of the narrative has Mary's body carried into Paradise while her soul is received into heaven, 'the treasure of the Father.' (Cf. Ernst, "Neues zur Kontroverse . . ." *Bonner Zeitschr.*, t. VI (1929), 295-296.)

[65] Cf. PO, t. 19, p. 370.

[66] Cf. Dom B. Capelle, "Les anciens récits de l'As-

123

somption et Jean de Thessalonique," *Recherches de théologie ancienne et médiévale,* t. xii (1940), p. 235.

[67] Cf. St. John Damascene, *In dormitionem B. M. Virginis, Hom.* i, 10, PG, 96, 716. Also: "We shall not call your holy passing death, but sleep or departure, or better still sojourn with God." *op. cit.,* 715; and: *"Your pure and spotless body has not been abandoned in the earth. But after your transference into* the royal abode of heaven, there you sit as queen, mistress, sovereign, true Mother of God." *op. cit.,* 720; finally: "O blessed Falling Asleep," writes St. Modestus, *"which knows not at all the decomposition of the tomb* because the all powerful Lord, Jesus Christ, has preserved untouched the flesh from which He was born." *Encomium in B. Virginem,* vii, PG, 86, 3294.

[68] In the thought of the Fathers Mary's maternity and virginity always refer to one another and flow into one another. In their argumentation in favor of the Assumption they never prescind completely from either one.

[69] Cf. St. Epiphanius, *Advers. Heares.,* 78, 18, PG, 42, 727.

[70] Cf. St. Germanus of Constantinople, *In dormit. B. Mariae,* Hom. ii towards the end, PG, 98, 347A.

[71] *op. cit.,* 361C (Hom. iii).

[72] Cf. John Damascene, *In dormit.,* Hom. ii, no. 3, PG, 96, 728.

[73] *op. cit.,* 725 (Hom. ii, no. 2).

[74] Cf. John Mauropos, *Serm. in SS. Deip. Dormit.,* 17-20, PG, 120, 1092.

[75] John 14, 3.

[76] See the same thought expressed by St. John Damascene, *In Dormit. B. V. Mariae,* Hom. ii, no. 3, PG, 96, 727.

[77] Cf. Pseudo-Augustinus, *De Assumptione Virginis*, 5 & 6, PL, 40, 1145s. Some similar reflections are found in Pierre de Celle (obit 1183), Serm. 68, *De Assumpt. B. M.*, PL, 102, 850s; and Pierre de Blois, Serm. 33, *In Assumpt. B. M.*, PL, 207, 661s. Cf. also J. B. Terrien, *La Mère de Dieu*, t. II, p. 384ss.

[78] Cf. *In Dormit.*, Hom. II, 14, PG, 96, 741.

[79] *ibid.*, 3, PG, 96, 728.

[80] *ibid.*, Hom. III, 5, PG, 96, 762.

[81] St. John Damascene, *In Dormit.*, Hom. I, 4, PG, 96, 706.

[82] Cf. St. Germanus of Constantinople, *In dormit.*, Hom. I, PG, 98, 248.

[83] Absalom Sprinchirsbacensis, Serm. 44, PL, 211, 255.

[84] Pseudo-Augustinus, *De Assumpt.*, 5, PL, 40, 1145.

[85] Bossuet, *Pour la fête de l'Assomption* (1660), edit. Lebarq-Urbain et Levesque, t. III, p. 489. This thought is already found in St. Modestus, *Encomium in B. V.*, VI, PG, 86, 3292s.

[86] Cf. St. Andrew of Crete, *In Dormit.*, Hom. II, PG, 97, 1081.

[87] Cf. St. Epiphanius, *Adversus Haereses*, 75, 8, PG. 42, 513 and Anacoratus, 100, PG, 43, 197 (edit. Holl. t. I, p. 120s).

[88] Cf. Denis the Carthusian, "De Praeconio et dignitate Mariae," art. III, *Opera Minora*, t. XXXV, p. 568 (edit. de Tournai)

[89] Canticle of Canticles, 8, 5.

[90] Cf. Pseudo-Damien, Serm. 40, *In Assumpt. B. M. V.;* St. Bernard, Serm. IV, *In Assumpt.;* Pierre de Blois, Serm. 33, *In Assumpt. B. M.;* Cornelius a Lapide, *Comment. in Cant.*, VIII, 5.

[91] Cf. J. Linden, "Die leibliche Aufnahme Mariä in den Himmel," *Zeitschr. f. kath. Theologie,* t. xxx (1906), pp. 215-221.

[92] Bossuet will say, "Our great Queen mounts to heaven leaning upon her Beloved. Worthy chariot of triumph! and well is she rewarded for the pain she had in carrying Him in her arms during His infancy. Surely, Holy Virgin, you lean indeed upon your Beloved, Him Who has drawn down on you all your glory; for His mercy is the fountain of all your merits." Cf. Bossuet, *Sermon pour la veille de l'Assomption* (1650), edit. Lebarq-Urbain et Levesque, t. i, p. 67.

[93] Cf. R. A. Lipsius, *Die apokryphen Apostelgeschichten,* t. i, pp. 445 & 500.

[94] Cf. Pseudo-Jerome, PL, 30, 123s ("plurimi asserverant").

[95] Cf. H. Delehaye, "Commentarius perpetuus," *Acta Sanctorum,* Nov., t. ii (1931), vi Kal. Jan. (December 27).

[96] Cf. Fulbert of Chartres, Serm. v, *De Nativitate V. M.,* PL, 141, 325.

[97] Cf. St. Modestus, *Encom. in Dormit.,* 6 & 7, PG, 86, 3292s.

[98] Cf. St. Germanus of Constantinople, *In Dormit.,* Serm. i, PG, 98, 345.

[99] Cf. St. John Damascene, *In Dormit.,* Hom. ii, 14, PG, 96, 741. Also the same homily, no. 3, *op. cit.,* 728.

[100] Cf. St. Theodore of Studium, *In Dormit.,* Hom. i, ii, PG, 99, 720, 724.

[101] Pseudo-Augustinus, *De Assumptione,* 6, PL, 40, 1145s. Also Denis the Carthusian, "De praeconio et dignitate Mariae," art. iii, *Opera Minora,* edit. de Tournai, t. xxxv (1898), p. 567s. And this is the excellent profession

of Pierre de Blois (obit 1204): "I believe that He Who in His birth kept intact the seal of His mother's virginity has Himself preserved from all corruption that virginal body where in Him the fulness of the Godhead has deigned to dwell. Yes! how would she,—how could she, who had lived completely chaste, completely immaculate, completely unspotted, without any stain of evil, suffer the decomposition of the body. She who on earth has led an angelic life can rise up to heaven in peace, leaving peace among men, strengthening their faith and assuring them of an everlasting charity." Serm. xxxiv, *De Assumptione*, PL, 207, 664.

[102] Romans, 8, 3.

[103] *De carne Christi*, 21.

[104] Matthew 22, 30.

[105] Cf. Tertullian, *De resurrectione carnis*, 26.

[106] Cf. St. Augustine, *De sancta virginitate*, 12.

[107] Apocalypse, 12, 1.

[108] Cf. Bossuet, *Sermon pour la fête de l'Assomption*, 2nd point, edit. Lebarq-Urbain et Levesque, t. iii, pp. 498-501.

NOTES TO CHAPTER THREE

[1] Such, for example, is the opinion of Zöckler. Cf. art. "Maria," *Realenzyklopädie f. prot. Theologie u. Kirche*, t. xii, p. 320.

[2] M. R. James, *The Apocryphal New Testament*, Oxford, 1924, pp. 194-227. See also A. Vitti, "Libri apocryphi de Assumptione B. M. V.," *Verbum Domini*, t. vi (1926), p. 225-234.

[3] Cf. Pseudo-Mileto, *Liber transitus Mariae*, cap. xvii, PG, 5, 1238.

[4] Cf. James, *op. cit.*, p. xix.

[5] Cf. Th. Zahn, *Acta Johannis*, p. 250.

[6] Cf. James, *op. cit.*, p. 197s. See also B. Capelle, "La fête de l'Assomption," *Ephemerides Lovan.*, t. iii (1926), p. 43s.

[7] Cf. James, *op. cit.*, p. 194.

[8] For example, we read in it of a curious descent into hell granted the Apostles. It was so popular as to spread even to Ireland, as St. J. Seymour shows. (Cf. James, *op. cit.*, pp. 219-226.)

[9] Cf. Gregory of Tours, *Miraculorum*, lib. i, "De gloria Martyrum," c. iv, PL, 71, 708. Also M. Jugie in *Echos d'Orient*, t. xxv (1926), p. 302s.

[10] Cf. A. Thiel, *Epistolae Romanorum Pontificum*, Brunsbergae (1868), p. 465.

[11] Cf. James, *op. cit.*, p. 195.

[12] Pseudo-Mileto, *De Transitu V. M.*, cap. ii, vi, viii, PG, 5, 1231-1240.

[13] The work has been published by M. Jugie in *Patrologie Orientale*, t. xix, pp. 375-405. See also M. Jugie, "Les premiers apocryphes sur la dormition," *Echos d'Orient*, t. xxv (1926), pp. 300-305.

[14] Cf. *Patrologie Orientale*, t. xix, p. 372.

[15] Cf. Epiphanius Monachus, *De vita B. Virginis*, viii, PG, 120, 214s.

[16] *ibid.*

[17] Cf. St. John Damascene, *In Dormit.*, Hom. ii, 18, PG, 96, 748ss. On this question consult M. Jugie, "Le récit de l'histoire euthymiaque sur la mort et l'Assomption de la Sante Vierge," *Echos d'Orient*, t. xxv (1926), pp. 385-392.

[18] Cf. infra, Appendix, pp. 101-103.

[19] The passage from the pseudo-Dionysius (*De divinis nominibus*, III, 2, PG, 3, 681), used first with reserve by Maximus the Confessor, more freely by St. Andrew of Crete (*In Dormit.*, Hom. I, PG, 97, 1064-1072), and then by the monk Epiphanius (cf. supra), is not sufficiently clear for it to be placed among the apocrypha on Mary's Falling Asleep. (Cf. M. Jugie, "Un texte du Pseudo-Denys l'Aréopagite," *Echos d'Orient*, t. xxv (1926), p. 305ss.)

[20] Cf. James, *op. cit.*, p. 201.

[21] Wright, *Contributions of the Apocryphal Literature*, London, 1865 (Syriac text and English translation), pp. 11-16; 42-51; 55-65.

[22] Cf. John of Thessalonica, *Dormitio Dominae Nostrae*, PO, t. 19, 376.

[23] Cf. Adamnan (623 or 624-704) reporting the testimony of the Bishop Arculf, who after his pilgrimage to the Holy Land had run aground in England. "That very frequent visitor to the Holy Land, St. Arculf, often visited the Church of the Holy Mary in the Valley of Josaphat . . . but within, on the righthand side is the stone sepulchre of the holy Mary, in which she rested for some time after her burial. But how or when or by whom her holy body was taken from the sepulchre, or where she awaits the resurrection, *they say that no one can know for certain.*" (*De locis sanctis*, edited by P. Geyer, CSEL, t. xxxviii, book I, chap. xii, p. 240.)

[24] Cf. St. Willibald (obit circa 787). "Starting out they come at last to the Valley of Josaphat where the sepulchre of the holy Mary is pointed out. But whether the Apostles buried her here when she was freed from the body, or whether after the sepulchre was dug out she was taken away with her body from those who meant to bury her, or once buried it is withdrawn; whether when it was

taken away it was placed somewhere else, or rose endowed with true immortality, *it is better to doubt than to determine anything about it according to the Apocrypha.*" Cf. "Vita," c. II, 12, *Acta Sanctorum,* July, t. II, p. 514.

[25] The Venerable Bede, influenced by Adamnan, writes on his part: "And on the right is the empty monument in which they say the holy Mary rested for a while; but by whom and when she was taken away is not known." Cf. *Liber de locis sanctis,* ed. of P. Geyer, CSEL, t. XXXIX, cap. v, p. 309. Cf. also *Retract. in Act. Apost.,* c. VIII.

[26] The pseudo-Ildefonsus is clearly influenced by the pseudo-Jerome. (Cf. Serm. v, PL, 96, 263s.) On the occasion of the feast of the Assumption it expresses itself as follows: "On that account let us glorify the *soul* of the Virgin magnifying the Lord (Luke 1, 46), which today Paradise takes up in joy." (*De Assumptione,* Serm. II, PL, 96, 252.) In Sermon VI his doubt about the *corporal* Assumption is still more clearly affirmed: "And we must not fail to mention what many welcome most willingly with the eagerness of piety: that on this day she was taken up in her body into the mansions of heaven by her Son, the Lord Jesus Christ. *But we should not assert all that may be piously believed, nor seem to accept as certain what is only doubtful.*" Cf. *De Assumpt.,* Serm. VI, PL, 96, 266s.

[27] Cf. T. A. Agius, "On Pseudo-Jerome," *Journal of Theological Studies,* t. XXIV (1923), pp. 176-183. See also D. C. Lambot, "L'homélie du pseudo-Jerome sur l'Assomption," *Revue bénédictine,* t. 46 (1934), p. 271.

[28] The letter of the pseudo-Jerome on the Assumption is found in PL, 30, 126-147. The passage cited is in 30, 124.

[29] Cf. Pseudo-Augustine, Serm. 208, *In festo Assumptionis B. M.,* PL, 39, 2130.

[30] Adon of Vienne, PL, 123, 202.

[31] The following is the text of Usuard: "The Church in her sobriety prefers piously to be ignorant of where God in His wisdom has hidden that venerable temple of the Holy Spirit, than to hold and teach anything frivolous and apocryphal." (PL, 124, 365.)

[32] PL, 131, 1142: "Because the most learned seem to disagree among themselves about these matters."

[33] Cf. PL, 194, 1862.

[34] Cf. Beleth, *Rationale*, c. 146, PL, 202, 148.

[35] Cf. Durandus of Mende, *Rationale*, book VII, c. XXIV, edit. of Lyon, 1551, p. 273.

[36] Cf. J. Ernst, *Bonner Zeitschr. f. Theologie und Seelsorge*, t. VI (1929), p. 297.

[37] See above all P. Hoffer, *La dévotion à Marie au déclin du* XVIIe *siècle*, Paris, 1928, p. 33s. Jansenism was so dangerous only because it allowed itself to be drawn down the same path.

[38] Cf. Benedict XIV, *De Festis Mariae V.*, Pars II, c. 116.

[39] Calude Joly, *De verbis Usuardi relatis in martyrologio parisiensi de Assumptione Beatae Virginis*, Sens, 1669. One year after this he published his *Epistola apologetica* addressed to the Cardinals of Retz and Bouillon, Rouen, 1670.

[40] Jacques Gaudin, *Assumptio corporea beatae Mariae virginis vindicata*, Paris, 1670. Nicolas Billiard, *Vindiciae parthenicae de vera Assumptione corporea beatae Mariae Virginis vindicata*, Sens, 1670.

[41] Cf. Benedict XIV, *De festis M. V.*, Pars II, c. 116.

[42] Cf. Tillemont, *Mémoires*, Brussels, 1732, t. I, p. 201, notes 9, 10, 11.

[43] *op. cit.*, t. I, p. 204, note 15.

131

[1] The Pope Sergius I solemnized the feast of the Assumption with a procession in the same way as the three other principal feasts of the Virgin, which leads one to suppose that for a certain number of years the Assumption had already had its place in the Roman liturgy. (Cf. Mgr. Duchesne, *Liber Pontificalis*, t. i, pp. 376 & 381, note 44.) See also Card. Schuster, *Liber Sacramentorum*, t. viii, pp. 42-53.

[2] Cf. P. M. Gordillo, *La Asuncion de Maria en la Iglesia Espanola*, Madrid, 1922.

[3] Cf. Dom Capelle, "La fête de L'Assomption," *Ephemerides theol. lovan.*, t. iii (1926), p. 35.

[4] "We left the Assumption of holy Mary for further inquiry." Cf. "Capitula ecclesiastica," no. 20, *Monumenta Germaniae*, Capitula Regum Francorum, edit. Boretius, t. i, p. 179.

[5] "We order to be celebrated as feast days during the year . . . the Assumption of holy Mary." Cf. the Council of Mayence, can. 36, *Concilia Germaniae*, t. i, p. 411.

[6] The Council of Clovesho ordered that feasts be celebrated exactly as in the Roman custom and rites. "Also that through the course of the whole year the birthdays of the saints (be celebrated) according to the martyrology of the same Roman Church, and on the same day." Cf. Council of Clovesho, no. 13, A. W. Haddan and W. Stubbs, *Councils and Ecclesiastical Documents Relating to Great Britain and Ireland*, Oxford, 1871, t. iii, p. 367.

[7] The feast is already mentioned by St. Boniface in his "Statuta," c. 34, Hartzheim, *Concilia Germaniae*, t. i, p.

75. And also by St. Chrodgang of Metz in his "Regula canonicorum," c. 74, Hartzheim, p. 118. Towards the year 800 it is prescribed by the Council of Salzburg (Capitula Regum Francorum, t. ı, p. 230, line 10), and for Basle by the Bishop Haiton (Capitula, t. ı, p. 363, line 40). Cf. also H. Jürgens, *Zeitschr. f. kath. Theologie*, t. ıv (1880), p. 627.

[8] Nicolas ı, *Ad consulta nostra*, PL, 119, 981.

[9] "He also decreed that the octave of the Assumption of holy Mary be celebrated in the Roman Church, which had not been done heretofore." Cf. Sigbert de Gembloux, *Chronica*, ad a. 847. Cf. also *Liber Pontificalis*, edit. Mgr. Duchesne, t. ıı, p. 112: "For he ordered that the octave day of the Assumption of the blessed Mother of God be celebrated with a vigil and matins, which had not been celebrated before."

[10] Cf. St. Bernard, *Epist.*, 174, 3, PL, 182, 333.

[11] Cf. Durandus of Mende, *Rationale*, 1. vıı, c. xxıv, edit. Lyon, 1551, p. 273.

[12] Cf. Suarez, *De Religione*, tract. ıı, 1. ıı, c. vııı, no. 8, in *Opera*, edit. Vivès, t. xııı, p. 283.

[13] Acts 1, 11 & Luke 24, 52.

[14] Cf. St. Cyprian, *Epist.*, x, 4, CSEL, edit. Hartel, p. 493, line 11. St. Gregory of Tours, *De Glor. Confess.*, c. 99. St. Augustine in his panegyrics uses the expression "the taking up of a bishop." See also J. Ernst, *Die leibliche Himmelfahrt Mariä*, p. 31.

[15] Cf. H. Delehaye, *Commentarius perpetuus in Martyrologium Hieronymianum ad recensionem H. Quentin*, Brussels, 1931, ad vı Kal. Jan. (December 27). With reference to this Thomassinus notes judiciously: "But it is my opinion according to the sentiment of believers, that St. John is not dead at all, but with his body has been

taken to some place of rest." Cf. *Traité des festes*, Paris, 1683, l. i. c. vii, no. 12.

[16] Nicholas of Clairvaux (the pseudo-Damian), Serm. *In Assumptionem beatissimae M. V.*, PL, 144, 717. "It is not likely," writes Suarez, "that assumption should be understood of the soul only, both because local assumption properly and strictly refers to the body, and because the souls of other saints also were taken up into heaven though the Church professes and celebrates no assumption for them, but only their passing over, their departure, their birthday." *De Mysteriis Vitae Christi* Disp. 21, Sect. ii, no. 5.

[17] The text is cited in a note taken from Roskovany, t. v, p. 545s, by S. Baümer, *Historie du bréviaire*, translated by Biron, Paris, 1905, t. ii, p. 379.

[18] Cf. Baümer, *ibid.*

[19] Cf. St. Gregory, *Liber sacramentorum*, xviii kal. Sept., PL, 78, 133.

[20] Abelard, Serm. 26, *De Assumptione beatae Mariae*, PL, 178, 541.

[21] Hildebert du Mans (*cenomanensis*), *In Assumptione B. Mariae*, PL, 171, 630.

[22] "But if this is true it follows that death is conquered and she has ascended in glory with her body." Cf. Salomon de Sprinckirsbach, Serm. 44, *In Assumpt. gloriosae Virginis*, PL, 211, 256.

[23] Cf. St. Albert the Great, *Quaest. super "Missus est,"* Quaest. 132, Opp. edit. Lyon, 1651, t. xx, p. 87s.

[24] Cf. Benedict xiv, *De festis B. M. V.*, Pars ii, c. 114, edit. 1758, p. 294. See also Suarez, *De Mysteriis Vitae Christi*, Dips. 21, sec. ii, no. 5; and Billuart, *Tractatus de Mysteriis Christi*, Dissert. xiv, art. ii, Prob. 1.

[25] Cf. *Missale gothicum*, "Missa in Adsumptione sanc-

tae Mariae Matris Domini nostri" (January), PL, 72, 245 & 246. St. Bernard makes admirable use of this idea of the two welcomes, the Incarnation and the Assumption, in his sermon on the Assumption, 3, PL, 183, 416. Bossuet also has made very happy use of it in the beginning of his sermon for the feast of the assumption. Edit. Lebarq-Urbain et Levesque, t. III, p. 488s.

[26] *Sacramentaire grégorien,* edit. Ménard, opera t. III, p. 123. Cf. PL, 78, 133.

[27] *Missale gothicum, loc. cit.* Let us recall here the text apparently belonging to St. John Damascene: "How would death have been able to devour her? . . . How would corruption have been able to attack the body in which Life was conceived?" (Orat. II, *In Dormit.*, PG, 96, 416.)

[28] Cf. B. Capelle, "La fête de l'Assomption," *Ephem. theol. lovan.,* t. III (1926), p. 40s.

[29] Cf. Benedict XIV, *De servorum Dei Beatificatione,* L. I, c. 42, no. 15.

[30] Cf. Bossuet, edit. Lebarq-Urbain, t. I, p. 63.

[31] Cf. *Liber Pontificalis,* edit. Mgr. Duchesne, t. I, p. 500.

[32] *op. cit.,* t. II, p. 61.

[33] Alexander III, Epist. XXII, in Labbé, t. XXI, p. 898, cited by J. Bellamy in the article "Assumption," DTC, t. I, col. 2133. Cf. PL, 207, 1077.

[34] The passage used in the breviary is found in PL, 30, 122.

[35] Lessons IV, V, VI of the feast of the Assumption. Oratio II, *de Dormitione B. M. V.,* post initum, PG, 96, 724-728, & sub finem *ibid.* 749.

[36] Cf. Ag. Lana, *La risurrezione e coroporea assunzione al cielo della S. Vergine, Madre di Dio,* p. 337.

[37] Cf. Benedict XIV, *De festis B. M. V.*, Pars, II, c. 114. See also Baronius, *Martyrologium romanum,* 2nd edit. Anvers, 1589, ad 15 August, note A, p. 361.

[38] The treatise is found in PL 40, 1141-1148.

[39] *loc. cit.,* 1147.

[40] *loc. cit.,* 1144. There is another text that can be cited: "For they are works of divinity that we speak of, and are therefore possible because they proceed from omnipotence. Moreover, Christ is the power of God and the wisdom of God, to Whom belong all things that are the Father's. *All things are which He wills to be, and He wills to be all that are upright and worthy. (loc. cit.,* 1143)

[41] *loc. cit.,* 1144.

[42] *ibid.*

[43] *loc. cit.,* 1148. In this argumentation there is nevertheless a gap. There is no allusion to the teaching of the Church, which is contained in the liturgical texts of the Gregorian Sacramentary and the Gothic Missal. Later, Abelard, Salomon of Sprinckirsbach and St. Albert the Great will begin to improve on this precious source of faith.

[44] Cf. for example Hugh of St. Victor, *Miscellanea,* 1. VI, c. 125, PL, 177, 808.

[45] Fulbert of Chartres, *De Nativitate Mariae Virginis,* PL, 141, 325.

[46] Hildebert du Mans: "Now today the blessed Virgin has obtained beatitude of soul and glorification of her body; and let us establish this by authority, *lest anyone should doubt it*." Cf. *In Assumptione B. M.,* Serm. I, PL, 171, 630.

[47] J. Beleth: "We know that this is true, that the blessed Mary has been assumed as far as her soul is concerned. But it is quite uncertain whether her body was also as-

sumed afterwards. *We piously believe, however,* that she was totally assumed; but first in soul, and then in body." Cf. *Rationale divinorum officiorum,* no. 146, PL, 202, 148.

[48] Cf. Sicard of Cremona: "As it is piously believed." Cf. *Mitrale,* c. 40, PL, 213, 420.

[49] Cf. Hugh of St. Victor, *loc. cit.,* PL, 177, 808.

[50] Cf. St. Albert the Great, *Quaest. super "Missus est,"* q. 132, in Opp. edit. Lyon, 1651, t. xx, p. 87s.

[51] Cf. St. Thomas, S. *Th.,* iii, q. 27, a. 1; also iii, q. 83, a. 5 ad 8.

[52] St. Thomas; "We believe that after death she was raised and carried into heaven." Cf. *In salutationem angelicam, vulgo "Ave Maria," expositio,* opera, edit. Parma, t. xvi, p. 134b.

[53] St. Bonaventure, Serm. i, *De Assumptione,* edit. Quaracchi, t. ix, p. 690a. Also Serm. ii, *De Assumptione, op. cit.,* p. 692a.

[54] Cf. Sicard of Cremona, *Mitrale,* c. 40, PL, 213, 420.

[55] Durandus of Mende: "It is to be believed piously that (Mary) was totally assumed." Cf. *Rationale,* 1. vii, c. 24, edit. Lyon, 1551, p. 272.

[56] Cited by H. Jürgens in *art. cit., Zeitschr. f. kath. Theologie,* t. iv (1880), p. 629.

[57] "Thirdly, she has been assumed with her risen body. This is piously believed by the faithful and confirmed by the doctors." Cf. S. *Theol.,* Pars iv, tit. 45, #5.

[58] Duplessis d'Argentré, *Collectio judiciorum,* t. i, p. 339s.

[59] Cf. Notger the Stammerer, *Martyrologium,* xvii kal. Sept., PL, 131, 1142. "Many among us doubt whether she was assumed together with her body, or left it and departed," declares the pseudo-Jerome (*Epist.* ix, no. 2, PL, 30, 123B). And as for himself, he does not regard it as

sufficiently proved to be believed, despite his desire to adhere to it (Cf. *loc. cit.*, 124). Ambrose Autpert, the pseudo-Augustine, is satisfied with admitting the possibility of the Assumption (Cf. pseudo-Augustine, Serm. 208, no. 2, PL, 39, 2130). At the end of the twelfth century the liturgist Beleth makes allusion to the vision of St. Elizabeth of Schönau, who confirms the Assumption, and declares: "It is quite uncertain whether the body of Mary was also assumed afterwards." Cf. *Rationale*, c. 146, PL, 202, 148.

[60] Cf. Aug. Deneffe, "Gualterii cancellarii et Bartholomaei Bononia, O. F. M., quaestiones ineditae de Assumptione B. V. M.," *Opuscula et textus*, series scholastica, fasc. IX, 1930, p. 11.

[61] *op. cit.*, p. 32.

[62] Cf. Gabriel Biel, "In festo Assumptionis B. M.," Serm. II, *Sermones*, edit. Cologne, 1619, pp. 347-351.

[63] *op. cit.*, Serm. III, p. 352.

[64] The thought of Gabriel Biel should be noted: "Thus her Son wished to undergo suffering and death for us, which are the consequences of sin, and to be subject to the law by which it is decreed that all men must die once. To this law His Mother was also subject." *op. cit.*, Serm. II, p. 344.

[65] *loc. cit.*, p. 348.

[66] *loc. cit.*, p. 347.

[67] *ibid.*

[68] *loc. cit.*, p. 348.

[69] *ibid.*

[70] *ibid.*

[71] *loc. cit.*, p. 349.

[72] *ibid.*

[73] *ibid.* & p. 350.

[74] *loc. cit.*, p. 350.

[75] Biel attributes the citation to St. Bernard. St. Bernard indeed expresses a similar idea (*Serm. in Nativitate B. M. V.*, 7, PL, 183, 441), but the expression itself is not found in his works. Without doubt the text is a fusion of two verses from Heb. 7, 25 and Luke 11, 27; its briefest form is: "The Son shows His wounds to the Father, and the Mother her breast to the Son," and it is found in many variants during the Middle Ages. It gave rise to the Plague Medals so common in Germany during the fifteenth century. Cf. S. Beissel, *Gesch. d. Verehrung Marias während des Mittelalters in Deutschland*, p. 358.

[76] Cf. *De locis theologicis*, 1. XII, c. 11; and *De Mysteriis Vitae Christi*, Disp. 21, sect. II, no. 9.

[77] *De Mysteriis* . . . , Disp. 3, sect. 6, no. 4.

[78] *ibid.*

[79] Cf. Catharinus, *Contra Cajetanum et opus de Conceptione* cited by Suarez, *De Mysteriis* . . . , Disp. 21, sect. II, no. 9.

[80] Cf. Steph. Beissel, *Geschichte der Verehrung Marias* . . . , Freiburg, 1909, p. 264.

[81] For Dominic Soto, cf. *In* IV *Sent.*, Dist. 43, q. 2, art. I ("to be believed most piously"). For Billuart, cf. *Tract. de Mysteriis Christi*, Dissert. 14, art. 11: "It would be rash to deny that the Blessed Virgin was assumed into heaven in both body and soul." And further on: "Who would deny that, to dare to impugn an opinion supported by so many authorities and reasons, and so honorable for the Mother of God, is to incur the *grave censure of rashness?*"

[82] This passage from St. Peter Canisius, taken from his great work on the holy Virgin, *De Maria Virgini incomparabili*, is cited by Benedict XIV to express his own opinion. Cf. *De festis B. M. V.*, Pars II, c. 120.

[83] Cf. *De Mysteriis* . . . , Disp. 21, sect. II, nos. 6-8.

[84] Cf. Legrand, "L'Assomption de Marie d'après l'enseignement des théologiens," *Congrès marial de Nantes,* 1925, p. 85. Also Ch. Duplessis D'Argentré, *Collectio judiciorum,* Paris, 1728, t. I, p. 339s.

[85] Cf. *De Assumptione,* art. 3, cap. 1, cited by C. Friethoff, "De doctrina Assumptionis corporalis B. M. V.," *Angelicum,* t. XV (1938), p. 5, note 1.

[86] Cf. De Bérulle, *Oeuvres de piété,* edit. Migne, col. 920. Also A. Molien, *Les grandeurs de Marie,* Paris, 1936, p. 525-537.

[87] Cf. Card. Bellarmine, Serm. 40, *De Assumptione B. M. V.,* edit. Cambrai, 1617, p. 329s.

[88] Cf. Théophile Raynaud, *Dypticha Mariana,* Pars II, punct. X, no. 2. Recall that Tillemont himself did not dare oppose this unanimous feeling, *Mémoirs,* Brussels, 1732, t. I, p. 206, note 15.

[89] Cf. *De Festis B. M. V.,* Pars II, c. 114.

[90] *loc. cit.,* c. 115.

[91] Cf. Glorie, *Discorso dell'Immacolata Concezione,* Punct. II.

[92] Cf. Sedlmayr, *Scholastica Mariana,* Pars III-VII, in Bourassé, *Summa Aurea,* t. VIII, col. 152.

[93] Cf. Trombelli, *Mariae sanctissimae vita et gesta,* Bononiae, 1763, t. IV, p. 371.

[94] Cf. H. Leclercq, "Assomption," DACL, t. I, col. 2991, fig. 1026.

[95] *loc. cit.,* col. 2984, fig. 1022.

[96] Ayala approves of this way of painting the Assumption although in reality Mary has no need of such help, since her risen body was gifted with a marvelous agility. Cf. *Pictor christianus eruditus,* lib. IV, c. VII, p. 210, edit.

Madrid, 1730. See also Suarez, *De Mysteriis* . . . , Disp. XXI, sect. II, no. 11, towards the end.

[97] Cf. Aug. Deneffe, "Gehört die Himmelfahrt Mariä zum Glaubensschatz?" *Scholastik,* t. III (1928), pp. 190-218.

NOTES TO CHAPTER FIVE

[1] Pius X, "Ad diem illum," ASS, t. XXXVI, p. 453.

[2] Cf. Martin, *Omnium concilii Vaticani quae ad doctrinam et disciplinam pertinent documentorum collectio,* II, pp. 112-121. Also P. Renaudin, *La doctrine de l'Assomption,* chap. VII, p. 189-204; and *Collec. lacensis,* t. VII, p. 869.

[3] Cf. Wiederkehr, *Die leibliche Aufnahme* . . . , Einsiedeln, 1927, pp. 114-118.

[4] *loc. cit.,* p. 119.

[5] Cf. E. Campama, *Maria nel dogma cattolico,* Turin, 1936, p. 808s.

[6] Cf. Ernst, *Die leibliche Himmelfahrt Mariä,* p. 8.

[7] Cf. Th. Livius, *The Blessed Virgin in the Fathers of the First Six Centuries,* London, 1893, p. 339.

[8] Cf. Scheeben, *Dogmatik,* t. III (1882), p. 579.

[9] Cited by Ernst in *Lintzer Quartalschr.,* t. 74 (1921), p. 383.

[10] Cf. Ernst, "Neues zur Kontroverse . . . ," *Bonner Zeitschr. f. Theologie u. Seelsorge,* t. VII (1930), pp. 18-21.

[11] Aug. Deneffe, "Gehört die Himmelfahrt . . . ?" *Scholastik,* t. III (1928), pp. 191-196.

[12] Cf. A. D. Sertillanges, *Mois de Marie,* Juvisy, 1935, p. 120. See also a beautiful passage on the Assumption, a

faithful mirror of traditional thought, in P. R. Bernard, *Le Mystère de Marie*, Paris, 1933, p. 306ss.

[13] "In a celebrated homily given to his people and clergy the Patriarch of Jerusalem, Cyril Lucaris, together with the 1672 Council of Jerusalem, give us the finest proofs that our brothers of the East acknowledge the triumph of Mary in her total Assumption no less than we." Cf. E. Campana, *Marie dans le dogme catholique*, translation of Viel, t. II, p. 554, Montréjeau, 1913. See also Cozza-Luzi, *De corporea Assumptione Beatae M. Deiparae testimonia liturgica graecorum selecta*, Rome, 1869; Passaglia, *De immaculato . . . conceptu*, sect. VI, art. I, no. 1488; Jürgens, "Kirchliche Uberlieferung," *Zeitschr. für k. Theologie*, t. IV (1880), p. 641s; and above all G. Hentrich et Rudolpho Gualtero de Moos, *Petitiones de Assumptione corporea B. V. M.*, t. II, pp. 855-878.

[14] If already at the end of the fifteenth century adhesion to the doctrine of the corporal Assumption was imposed on the faithful under pain of mortal sin—and the retraction demanded of the Dominican John Morcelle shows that this was so—, then the doctrine demands today an adhesion even more firm, as being founded on an agreement more universal and unanimous.

[15] Cf. Mgr. Malou, *L'Immaculée Conception de la Bienheureuse Vierge Marie*, Brussels, 1857, t. II, p. 514. So as not to create misunderstanding we wish to state our position exactly. We do not at all say that the text from Genesis, *taken alone*, tells that Mary in intimate union with Christ wins a complete victory over Satan; nor do we say even that *it can be proved* that patristic and theological tradition have read this meaning into the text. We say only that the *ordinary magisterium of the Church*, specifically Pius IX's emphatic declaration, *while leaning*

142

upon this text from Genesis, represents Mary to us as indissolubly united with Christ and hence as the New Eve, and as winning a total victory with Him and by Him over Satan and over sin. It is this assertion of the ordinary magisterium that serves as the basis of our whole argumentation.

[16] Cf. St. Justin, *Dialogue contre Tryphon*, no. 100. Cf. also Rouët de Journel, *Enchridion Patristicum*, Index theologicus, no. 433; and Scheeben, *Dogmatik*, t. III, p. 592s.

[17] Cf. Wiederkehr, *Die leibliche Aufnahme* . . . , pp. 156-159.

[18] Cf. Scheeben, *loc. cit.*, p. 584.

[19] Cf. Card. Zigliara, *Summa philosophica*, t. I, p. 516s.

[20] Cf. Scheeben, *loc. cit.*, p. 601.

[21] Cf. St. Augustine, *De Trinitate*, 1. IV, c. 14; St. Thomas, *Summa*, III, q. 30, a. 1.

[22] Genesis 2, 17. 19; 3, 14.

[23] If Mary has died, it is not at all because she has fallen under the chastisement placed by God on the race of Adam. Quite the contrary, her fulness of grace assures her a right to immortality. But if Mary has not enjoyed the use of this right, this is because of the "economy of our salvation" which centers around the redemptive death of the divine Saviour. Mary had to give birth to a pure, human and mortal flesh, says St. Thomas following St. Augustine. (*Summa*, III, q. 48, a. 3, ad. 1.) This implies the possibility of death for the Virgin. But if the Redemption, as God had planned it, demanded the death of Mary —at least through a miraculous and abnormal intervention—as it demanded that of the God-Man Himself, it does not in any way call for a prolonged sojourn in the tomb. Once this obstacle has been overcome, the right to

immortality ought to come into play for Mary's benefit and assure her of a resurrection and corporal Assumption.

[24] Cf. *Collect. lacens.*, VII, 869.

NOTES TO CHAPTER SIX

[1] Cf. Campana, *Maria nel dogma cattolico*, Turin, 1936, p. 898s.

[2] At present the two volumes which the Jesuits Guillaume Hentrich and Raoul Gautier de Moos have just published under the eyes of, and with the approbation of the Sovereign Pontiff, show in striking fashion the sweep of the movement that is carrying souls towards Mary and makes them long to see the corporal Assumption of the Mother of God proclaimed as an article of faith. (*Petitiones de Assumptione corporea B. V. Mariae in caelum definienda ad S. Sedem delatae, propositae secundum ordinem hierarchicum, dogmaticum, geographicum, chronologicum, ad consensum Ecclesiae manifestandum*, Libreria Vaticana, 2 vol., pp. XLIV+1064 & XVI+1110.) And new series of petitions begin to flow to Rome.

[3] Cf. Ernst, *op. cit.*, p. 8.

[4] Cf. Wiederkehr, *op. cit.*, p. 146.

[5] *op. cit.*, p. 147.

[6] Cf. Mgr. Malou, *L'Immaculée Conception de la Bienheureuse Vierge Marie*, Brussels, 1857, t. II, p. 381ss.

[7] Cf. Campana, *Marie dans le dogme chrétien*, translated by Viel, t. II, p. 589.

[8] Cf. *Marianum*, t. VIII (1946), p. 184.

[1] Cf. the bibliography of Marian art at the beginning of our article "Le visage de Marie à travers les siècles, dans l'art religieux," *Nouvelle Revue Théologique,* mai-juin 1946, p. 282. Also K. Künstle, "Tod und Verherrlichung Marias," *Ikonographie der chirstlichen Kunst,* Freiburg, 1928, t. i, pp. 563-583; J. Helbig, "La mort et la résurrection de la Sainte Vierge," *Revue de l'art chrétien,* t. 37, 1894, p. 367ss.; C. Jéglot, *La vie de la Vierge dans l'art,* Paris, 1927; E. Male, *L'art religieux du xiiie siècle en France,* Paris, 1906, p. 248ss.

[2] Acts 1, 11.

[3] Psalm 17, 17.

[4] Cf. Le Blant, *Sarcophages d'Arles,* plate xxxiii, no. 2. Also H. Leclercq, "Ascension," DACL, t. i, col. 2928, fig. 987.

[5] Leclercq, *loc. cit.,* col. 2929, fig. 988.

[6] Leclercq, "Assomption," *loc. cit.,* col. 2991, fig. 1026.

[7] Cf. Garrucci, *Storia dell'arte cristiana,* plate 178, no. 7.

[8] Cf. Leclercq, "Pierre," DACL, t. xiii, col. 939, fig. 10220.

[9] *loc. cit.,* col. 944, fig. 10226.

[10] *ibid.,* fig. 10227.

[11] Cf. G. Llopart, "Los origenes de la creencia y de la fiesta de la Asunción in Espana," *Estudios Marianos,* t. vi, 1947, p. 155ss.

[12] Luke 24, 52.

[13] Leclercq, "Ascension," DACL, t. i, col. 2927, fig. 985.

[14] *loc. cit.,* plate inserted in the text.

[15] Leclercq, "Ampoules," DACL, t. i, fig. 458-460.

[16] Cf. pseudo-Melito, *Transitus,* c. xviii. See also James, *The Apocryphal New Testament,* p. 216, and p. 196 where it is told that a variant of the Coptic narrative had already reported thus: "And Peter and John and all of us looked on while she *was carried to heaven* until she was lost from view."

[17] Cf. *Revue de l'art Chrétien,* ive série, t. viii, 1897, p. 227ss.; Leclercq, "Assomption," DACL, t. i, col. 2984, fig. 1022.

[18] Cf. *Liber Pontificalis,* edit. Mgr. Duchesne, t. i, p. 500.

[19] *op. cit.,* t. ii, p. 61.

[20] Cf. A. Michel, *Histoire de l'art,* t. i, part ii, p. 289, S. Beissel, *Geschichte der Verehrung Marias während des Mittelalters in Deutschland,* p. 89, fig. 35.

[21] Cf. pseudo-Melito, *De transitu V. Mariae,* c. ix, PG, 5, 1235.

[22] Cf. John of Thessalonica, "Dormito Deminae nostrae," PO, t. 19, p. 396.

[23] Cf. Vöge, *Malerschule,* p. 8 & 12, note 2.

[24] Cf. Beissel, *Geschichte der Verehrung . . . ,* p. 194, fig. 91.

[25] Cf. *Zeitschrift f. christliche Kunst,* t. iii, 1890, p. 143ss.

[26] Cf. Beissel, *loc. cit.,* p. 193s.

[27] Cf. I. F. Robinson, "Boharic Accounts of the Falling Asleep of Mary with Saidic Fragments," *Texts and Studies,* t. iv, no. 2, p. 65, Cambridge, 1896.

[28] Cf. pseudo-Melito, *De transitu . . . ,* cc. xvi-xviii, PG, 5, 1238s. In the *Golden Legend* Jacopo de Voragine reproduces exactly the text of the pseudo-Melito under

August 15. See the translation by Th. de Wyzewa, Paris, 1911, p. 434s.

[29] Cf. E. Male, *L'art religieux du* XIIIe *siècle* . . . , p. 246, fig. 124 and p. 254s. Also *Notre-Dame de Paris,* edit. "Tel," plates 23 & 24.

[30] Cf. E. Male, *op. cit.,* p. 255.

[31] Cf. M. Jugie, "Le récit de l'histoire euthymiaque . . . ," *Echos d'Orient,* t. xxv, 1926, pp. 385-392.

[32] This narrative is attributed to Joseph of Armathea. Cf. James, *op. cit.,* p. 217s. Also Künstle, *Ikonographie* . . . ," t. i, p. 583.

[33] Emile Male points out a minature of the thirteenth century, copied by the Comte de Bastard, which treats our subject. Cf. p. 256.

[34] Cf. K. Künstle, *op. cit.,* t. i, p. 582, no. 327.

[35] Cf. F. A. Gruyer, *Les Vierges de Raphaël,* t. ii, Paris, 1869, p. 563ss.

[36] For the engraving of Dürer see Künstle, *op. cit.,* t. i, p. 576, no. 323.

[37] A beautiful reproduction of Orcagna's work is found in Künstle, *loc. cit.,* no. 329.

[38] The Assumption of the chevet of Notre Dame in Paris is reproduced in *Notre-Dame de Paris,* edit. "Tel" fig. 11 (fourteenth century), and in E. Male, *op. cit.,* p. 247, fig. 125.

[39] Cf. A. Michel, *Hist. de l'art,* t. ii, part ii, p. 648 (end of the fifteenth century).

[40] At Magdeburg the sculptor has had the bad taste to place the Virgin, framed in the oval nimbus, on a litter covered with draperies, which two angels carry. Cf. A. Michael, *op. cit.,* t. ii, part ii, p. 752.

[41] For Donatello's work see Michel. *op. cit.,* t. iii, part ii, p. 565.

[42] Cf. Laforge, *La Sainte Vierge*, p. 272, and Rothes, *Die Madonna*, 2nd edition, fig. 160.

[43] It is quite exceptional that Albert Bouts (obit 1549) represents Mary as carried towards the Father by the other two Persons of the Trinity. His picture, a triptych, is in the Brussels Museum.

[44] Cf. F. X. Kraus, *Geschichte der christlichen Kunst*, t. ii, part ii, p. 739s. See also *Newnes' Art Library*, "The Early Work of Titian," plates 50-53, London.

[45] Cf. Beissel, *op. cit.*, pp. 379-382.

[46] The Assumption was one of the religious subjects that responded best to an artistic genius drunk with life, light and space. Among the most successful works we cite the Assumptions of the Cathedral of Anvers, the Brussels Museum, the Lichtenstein Gallery (Vienna) and the Colonna Gallery (Rome).

[47] Cf. Michel, *op. cit.*, t. iii, part ii, p. 564.

Brief Bibliography

I—Bibliographical Table

Carlo Passaglia, *De Immaculato Deiparae semper Virginis conceptu, sec.* VI, c. VI. The *"De Immaculato . . ."* is one of the very finest sources of references and citations for the question that concerns us. Certain texts, however, demand a critical attitude more severe and delicate before they can be useful.

J. Scheeben, *Handbuch der Katholischen Dogmatik,* t. III, p. 570ss.

B. H. Merkelbach, *Mariologie.* Paris, 1939, p. 272, note 1: Bibliographie des auteurs les plus récents.

Cl. Dillenschneider, *La Mariologie de saint Alphonse de Liguori—Source et synthèse doctrinale,* Fribourg, 1934. Short resume of the opinions of theologians from St. Thomas to the present day.

F. Cavallera, *Patrologiae cursus completus . . . series graeca,* Indices, pp. 166-167: *In Dormitionem.* He points out the homilies of the Greek Fathers on the Dormition of Mary.

II—Source Works

The Pseudo-Augustine, *De Assumptione B. V. M.*, liber unus, PL, 40, 1141-1148. This treatise should not be confused with an apocryphal sermon also attributed to St.

Augustine, which is perhaps by Ambrose Autpert, an adversary of the corporal Assumption; Sermo 208, PL, 39, 2129-2134.

St. Canisius, *De Maria Virgine incomparabili,* 1. v, c. 5, in J. Bourassé, *Summa aurea* . . . t. ix, p. 62ss.

Suarez, *De Mysteriis vitae Christi,* disp. 21, sec. 1ss.

Benedict xiv, *De Festis B. M.,* Pars ii, c. cix-cxxvi; and *De canonisatione sanctorum,* i, xlii, 15.

J. C. Trombell, SS. *Mariae vita et gesta,* sec. i, dissert. 45, in J. Bourassé, *Summa aurea,* t. ii, p. 287ss.

Agostino Lana, *La Risurrezione e corporea Assunzione al cielo della* S. *Vergine Madre di Dio,* Rome, 1880.

J. Scheeben, *Dogmatik,* t. iii, p. 578-588.

P. Renaudin, *La doctrine de l'Assomption de la Très Sainte Vierge, sa définibilité comme dogme de foi,* Paris, 1913.

―――, *Assumptio B. Mariae Virginis Matris Dei, disquisitio theologica,* Turin, 1933. This work takes up and completes the preceding. "The abundant testimony of the Fathers and theologians (pp. 35-99) would have profited by being presented in a more critical way." (E. Druwé)

J. B. Terrien, *La Mère de Dieu,* t. ii, 1. viii, pp. 317ss.

Guido Mattiussi, *L'Assunzione corporea della Vergine Madre di Dio,* Milan, 1924. Recasting and translation of the work of the same writer, *Utrum corporea Virginis Assumptio ad fidei depositum spectet?,* Aquipendii, 1922.

M. Favier, *L'Assomption corporelle de la Mère de Dieu dans le dogme catholique,* d'après les travaux du R. P. Guido Mattiussi, Paris, 1926. Adaption and popularisation of the work of Father Mattiussi.

Congrès marial de Nantes. This convention took the corporal Assumption of Mary as its special theme. Among the works presented note above all those of V. Bainvel, *La définibilité de l'Assomption,* and of Le Grand, *L'Assomption selon les théologiens.* Cf. Resume of the Convention in E. Campana, *Maria nel culto cattolico,* Turin, 1933, pp. 729-732.

P. Wiederkehr, *Die leibliche Aufnahme der allerseligsten Jungfrau Maria in den Himmel,* Einsiedlen, 1927.

M. Jugie, *La mort et l'Assomption de las Sainte Vierge,* historical and doctrinal study in the collection "Studi e Testi," no. 114, Vatican City, 1944.

Petitiones de Assumptione corporea B. V. Mariae in caelum definienda ad S. Sedem delatae, propositae secundum ordinem hierarchicum, dogmaticum, geographicum, chronologicum ad consensum Ecclesiae manifestandum, by Guglielmo Hentrich and Rudolpho Gualtero de Moos, Vatican Library, 2 vols., xliv+1064; xvi+1110 pp. In this important work see in particular: t. ii, pp. 855-879 (The testimony of the East); t. ii, pp. 661-773 (Theological qualification); t. ii, pp. 880-1039 (History of the development of belief in the Assumption from 1863 to 1940).

III—Articles from Journals

H. Jürgens, "Die kirchliche Ueberlieferung von der Aufnahme der Gottesmutter in den Himmel," *Zeitschr. für kathol. Theologie,* t. iv (1880), pp. 595-650.

J. Linden, "Die leibliche Aufnahme Mariä in den Himmel," *Zeitschr. für kathol. Theologie,* t. xxx (1906), pp. 201-207.

Aug. Deneffe, "Gehört die Himmelfahrt Mariä zum Galubensschatz?" *Scholastik,* t. iii (1928), pp. 190-218.

C. Friethoff, "De doctrina Assumptionis corporalis B. Mariae Virginis, rationibus theologicis illustrata," *Angelicum,* t. xv (1938), pp. 3-16.

151

C. Balic, "De definibilitate Assumptionis B. Virginis Mariae in caelum," *Antonianum,* t. xxi (1946), pp. 3-67.

IV—*The Assumption and the Liturgy*

E. Campana, *Maria nel culto cattolico,* Turin, 1933, t. i, pp. 350-382 (The Feast of the Assumption.)

Cozza-Luzi, *De Corporea Assumptione Beatae Mariae Deiparae testimonia liturgica graecorum selecta,* Rome, 1869.

Card. Schuster, "La fête de l'assomption de la Bienheureuse Vierge au ciel dans la liturgie romaine," *Liber sacramentorum,* t. viii (1932), pp. 41-56.

B. Capelle, "La fête de l'Assomption dans l'histoire liturgique," *Ephemerides theologicae Lovanienses,* t. iii (1926), pp. 33-45.

R. Bernard, "L'Assomption et la Maternité de grâce," *Vie spirituelle,* t. xxviii (1931), pp. 28-51.

V—*Some Adversaries of the Corporal Assumption of Mary*

Claude Joly, *De verbis Usuardi relatis in Martyrologio parisiensi de Assumptione Beatae Virginis,* Sens, 1669.

Launoy, *Judicium de controversia super exscribendo parisiensi ecclesiae martyrologio exorto,* 1671.

J. Ernst, *Die leibliche Himmelfahrt Mariä,* historisch-dogmatisch nach ihrer Definierbarkeit beleuchtet, Regensburg, 1921.

Since these pages have been written numerous works on the Assumption have been published. We note the most important of these:

J. M. Bover, "La Asunción de Maria en el 'Transitus' y en Juan de Tesalonica," in *Estudios eclesiasticos*, t. xxx (1946), pp. 415-433.

J. Coppens, "La définibilité de l'Assomption," in *Ephemerides theologicae Lovanienses*, 1947, pp. 5-35.

F. Cayré, "La définibilité de l'Assomption de Maria, à propos d'un livre récent" (the book of Father Jugie), in *L'Année Théologique*, 1946, pp. 373-399.

O. Faller, "De piorum saeculorum silentio circa Assumptionem B. Mariae Virginis," in *Analecta Gregoriana*, t. xxxvi (series facultatis theologicae, sec. A, no. 5), 1946.

P. Gasso, "Sobre los origenes de la fiesta de la Asunción," in *Estudios Marianos*, t. vi (1947), pp. 138-146.

M. Gordillo, "L'Assunzione corporale della SS. Vergine Madre di Dio nei teologi bizantini" (sec. x-xv), in *Marianum*, t. ix (1947), pp. 64-89.

G. Llopart, "Los origenes de la creencia y de la fiesta de la Asunción en Espana," in *Estudios Marianos*, t. vi (1947), pp. 155-198.

F. S. Müller, "Petitiones de Assumptione corporea B. V. Mariae in caelum definienda," in *Gregorianum*, t. xxvii (1946), pp. 110-135.

Archangelus a Roc, "Adnotationes circa Petitiones de B. V. Mariae Assumptione corporea in caelum dogmatice definienda," in *Collectanea Franciscana*, t. xiv (1944), pp. 260-311.

E. Bayerri, "El misterio de la Asunción de Maria en la liturgia hispana medieval," in *Estudios Marianos*, t. vi (1947), pp. 381-402.

G. Braso, "Contenido doctrinal de las formulas asuncionistas de la liturgia romana," in *Estudios Marianos*, t. vi (1947), pp. 147-154.

The
Glorious Assumption

Translated from the French by

Joan Maxwell Travers, S.J.

Catholics have through the ages believed in the Assumption of the Blessed Mother, even though the doctrine had never been proclaimed as a matter of revealed truth. Now in this "Age of Mary," when Catholics by the millions are turning to Our Lady for consolation, the Holy Father has seen fit to define the truth de fide. Belief in the Assumption now becomes a matter of dogma.

This proclamation, coming in the Holy Year of 1950, was not unexpected. In fact, it was in anticipation of the definition that the original French edition of The Glorious Assumption was written. Furthermore, the translator, a theologian of Wood-

tells the amassed evidence, theological in its style, instead of enhances greatly ... the story of The Mother of God.